Whispers of the Witch by NanyWytch

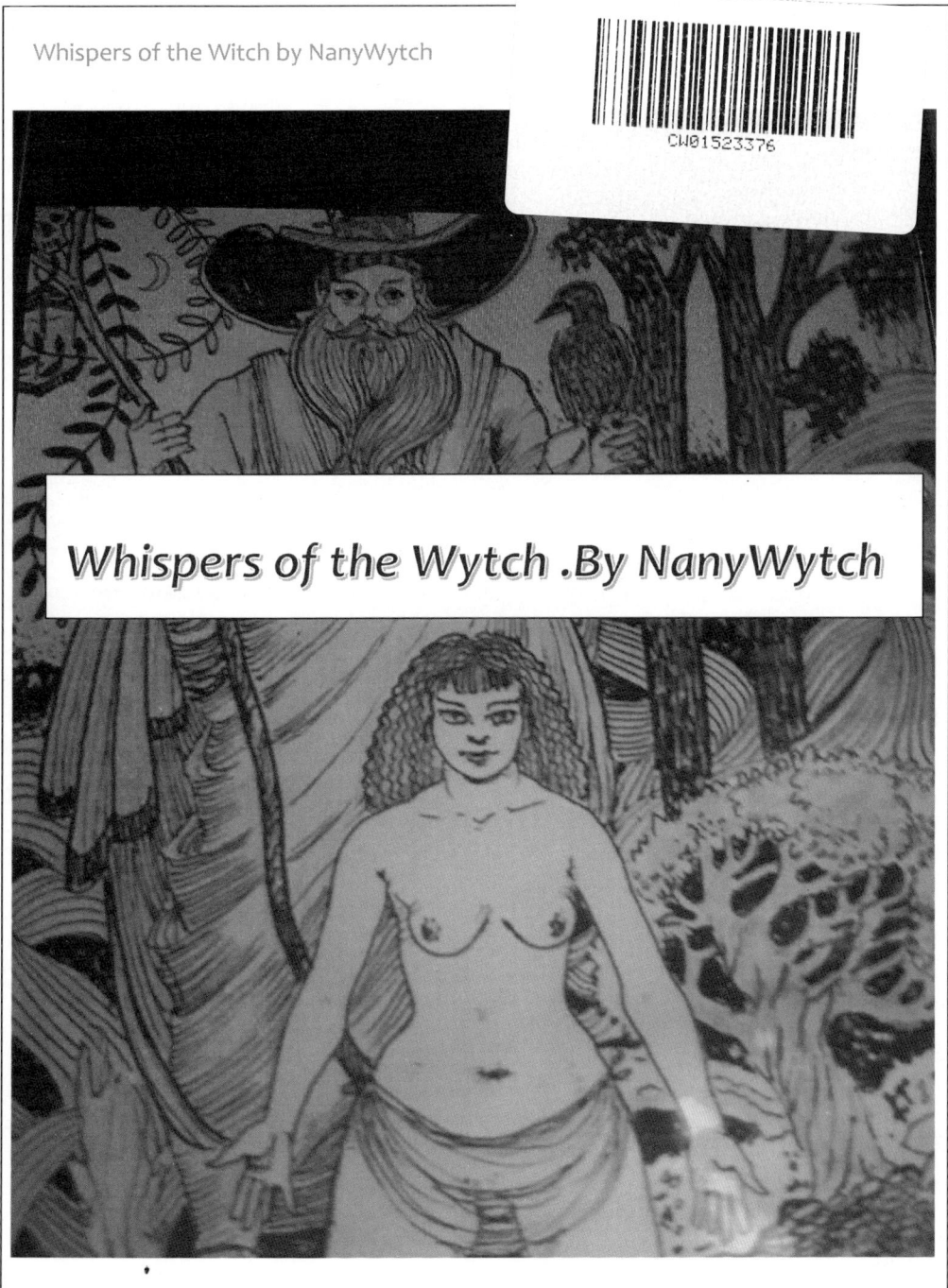

Whispers of the Wytch .By NanyWytch

copyright Ashna Yates BSC 2020

Copyright

Copyright NanyWytchWriter.co.uk 2020

This is a work of nonfiction, memories of a wytch with over 42 years experience. Names have been altered for privacy of persons.

The moral right of the author has been asserted.

All rights reserved

Without limiting rights under copyright no part of this publication may be reproduced, stored or introduced into a retrieval system, or transmitted in any form or by any means (electronic, mechanical or otherwise) without prior written consent of the author and publisher of this book.

Dedicated to

Mark my husband and best mate

My four children of whom I am very proud

RBB for the teachings he gave me

Owen for sharing his African heritage teaching me about voodoo

An Authors note

Tis best to die on your feet than live a life on your knees.

I make no apologies for what is written as they are true factual accounts from my life.

The past cannot be changed only learnt from. This book is not like others written by a witch I will not tell you how to walk your path.

I will say having spent every day where I spoke to the gods and spirit has given me a quite different perspective.

I was taught that there are 3 main conditions of humanity on earth, those who sleep questioning nothing for its not yet their time. It is cosmic law they are not disturbed as those Who are woken ones who search for their path through life seeking knowledge in different degrees and stages. They are hungry for wisdom and knowledge they must be looked after guided where possible. Those who are the advanced ones who share their knowledge with others that they may learn.

Where there are woken ones there are also wolves & carrion these feed on these innocents, claiming they are priests of some cult or other, be thee cautious if your instincts say No do not do it, they tell true.

First, I ask nobody to believe what they themselves cannot grasp with their own minds. The importance is that you read with an open mind.

I have dwelled in the daylight of the Gods so how I see things might not yet be in your understanding of the magical realms most of my own teaching came from several teachers.

Too much water you can drown, too much air you live in illusion, too much fire you burn out quicker, too much earth you stagnate and die.

High magick opens your eyes to other dimensions all around us, that cannot be comprehended by weak or fearful persons. Not because it can scare the crap out of you. Because it demands study, time, effort, dabblers cannot paddle in deep water there are no arm bands once the door is opened.

Magick affects you on 3 planes physical, astral & mental, it changes you.

Make sure you are comfortable in your own skin, to be perfectly honest with thyself. Everybody including myself has a past. Your fears are created from some trauma in your life or the past lives try to find what they were so your own demons do not plague you. We all have them to some degree.

Magick demands complete focus, absolute discipline, tenacity and courage when done correctly it will create a profound change in yourself.

High magick roots go as far back as ancient Egypt, ancient Greece. Most high magick scrolls were in Greek before being translated to Latin. The aim is to effect change in your inner and outer selves shaping the unseen energies of the earth. There is no black or white magick the power is neutral only you can colour its form.

But then I know nothing

NanyWytch 2020.

WHISPERS OF THE WYTCH

By

NANYWYTCH

Whispers of the Witch by NanyWytch

Preface

Letter to my Magus

Canst tha see em when they are dead?

The picture in the hall

War hero

Whispering walls

Authors note

Sowen

Sealed letter

They are all pagans here

Far field

Screeching trees

Stone the wytch

Mirror on the wall

Playing with Demons can harm

Dolls House Bedford

Potion called Anaesthesia

Rytes in the wood

Hekomya

Chalk & board rubber

Glenworth Manor

Dem'orai

Hollow Whispers

Raped by a god

Lodge Street

Darker times

Voodoo

Stone henge

Talagmar

Sonia

Visions

1070

Astral projection

Hardman Street

Midsummer Madness

Sweet demon

Woodcut picture of RBB my Magus.

All artwork in this book are original works done by RBB for me.

Preface

If said I was born this way, what does that actually mean? Simply that I am not like you being different was not easy, because in our world if you stand outside of what is considered to be the Norm. You remain outside looking in often wishing to not have these gifts.

Growing up where you were different meant at first you thought you were broken, needed fixing my family thought this or rather my father a staunch Methodist did.

You did not know why you could see spirits, were an empath and psychic you had this uncanny connection to animals; they would come to you, you would know what they needed how you did not question. You felt your way into the realms of spirit, being this way meant you held spirit above body.

To you it felt lonely living with creatures who feared you, kept you apart from them. Because of the way you saw the world. Yet the Gods would speak directly to you.

With parents brought up in the Christian ethos they did not know what they were doing, they believed the priests that I was infected by Satan. They did not know that those priests could not talk to angels and spirits, so they told my parents something was wrong with me. They did not know this concept was tainted by the very church they listened to. Over the years the church had changed things to give them all the power. Removing from the people their contact with the nature spirits of their heritage.

Creating a devil in 1484 to blame for the evil men do. The people instead now sat in empty cold buildings seeking the contact they needed spiritually. But this white Christ God king deemed them unworthy to even attend so this invisible presence was worshipped.

Those who were born different were pushed away yet at the same time called upon, by the very same people who shunned them for healing potions and spells. These witches and shamans did what they knew how to do. But after doing so were hunted out and killed because the church said they were tainted by evil. They got rid of all female aspects because they feared she was different; she was meant to feel she was wrong for being born this way.

In 1645 they tried to drown me then hung me from a bridge because I could make healing potions. Help women deliver babies.

Now I have lived this life different from even my own family, like looking through a mirrors reflection I have decided to share my memories with you. My way may not be yours, but I ask you to simply read and learn from these experiences all you can.

Letter to a Magus

Whispers of the Witch by NanyWytch

Letter to my Magus

I recall our first meeting as if it were yesterday, yet some 32 years have lapsed. I needed aid from someone with power I had been told to return in one hour, on my return I was asked by the shop owner Chris to pass him a book amidst his crowded shelves, I knew his shelves wellbeing a regular customer there, so I knew exactly where to lay my hands on that book.

As I reached out your hand took mine, you spoke very gently, your eyes were vivid and alive. Your hair greying your wisdom showing in your eyes, you asked for the keys to another room and they were given this was on a crowded Saturday afternoon they were passed in silence.

We walked to this place I noticed that everyone looked and that some had envy in their eyes. You asked where I was staying, I said a hotel you said you could, not protect me from there that I needed to come to your place, you must have seen my thoughts because you answered before I asked. That day I came to your home for the first time as we waited for the attack to come in your temple that night, you did a rite in Latin I did not understand more than a few words.

I was an initiated wytch, you a Magi our paths so distinct and yet so different yet the same in some ways, you had sworn an oath to ISIS I to Diana, two ancient Goddesses two hugely different ways.

From that point you began to teach me I stayed with you many times now as much as life could offer, you took me to places had never been oft you would scold me but your eyes always shined, once you took me to a wood with others of your path to perform a rite. I was the only witch the rest were male and all on the path of the Magus. Whilst one of the males pre-occupied me with a game of geometric sigils in the earth a test of who is better at magick you and the others cast a circle, built a fire, a throne and made a crown from things of the earth and trees

You called me to come take my place on the throne to be the queen of the rite, I refused saying I was busy, I did not much feel like a queen today. You summoned me as leader to come!! I was in circle I cried out I was doing this under duress.

You crowned me I sat on this throne you bowed before me giving me the power of this circle your sword, you asked me to bless the participants of the rite we told you I could not possibly, as I did not quite feel like blessing people today

I had seen with magical eyes the persons within I had seen jealousy, envy, and those who would kiss your arse if you asked them too.

You told me to throw the crown into the ritual fire as I did not deserve to be queen then I refused You told me to return your sword and the power of the circle I knew you could, harm me but I did not care I sat there so defiant and as our eyes met you saw what was there, I had to know if you were as they.

You smiled at me as I said you gave it to me you take it from me, but the challenge was not from me but from my Lady you saw her with me

You simply dismantled the circle around me, then I returned your sword to you disappearing into the woods. I was not far away, I heard the things they said to you if she were my acolyte, she would not speak to me with such disrespect after all that is what you get teaching a mere witch!

All you said was keep to the path, my Lady showed me in the stream later that day told me not to be there. I went straight to your willow tree giving it the crown and telling it to take good care of it

(And it did)

They all slagged me off and you asked me to make the tea saying acolytes make the drinks as I served it to everyone around the room, I told them that I had put belladonna or henbane in copious amounts in their drinks of all those in the room only you drank from your cup.

Only you trusted they feared you sent me away to write up the seven rays sometimes later you hugged me and said I had passed I never understood what!

Over the years that have passed you have shared my happiness, my pain, my growth, and my renewal.

When I walked in the dark and none would aid me you reached out your hand and I came home

But now in these late years my light is bright whilst yours grows dim, yet you I would trust you with my very soul often did.

You taught me magic's, evocation, invocation, transfiguration, and over enshadowment, understanding, perseverance, discretion, and silence.

You showed me the world of possession, of night and of Demons, you taught me of Angels and of light, you saw in me what others feared yet no one had ever come this close before You gave of yourself without question, you never lied to me even if I would not like what you told me, you had the ability to see right through me and none knew how much I loved thee

Once when I summoned a Demon that came, I scared myself shitless for I had left the rite without Where would I have been without you, you sent a summoner you lectured me about why not to evoke Demons the words you yelled at me still today have power

When you are as good as the dust under my sandals you will have learnt something of the realities of truth and magick's

As my mentor you blocked my mirror for three whole moons, denied me any magic's meditations, contact with like mind, preventing me from doing anything that was of the way of the Wyrd

You sealed my temple against me and bid me do penance you took away all my toys,

I threw all my teddies out the cot

This was my worst nightmare NO magic's to make me feel safe, no spirits to talk to, no physical contact with those of like mind I drove nearly everyone around me crazy as I yearned for my life back (I could not be normal ordinary, Christian even AHHHh)

When my own coven met without me, I wanted so to go but I knew I could not

But when that third moon rose in its sky, I broke the seal, and I went inside my temple I shouted at you through my mirror to get the hell out of my mirror…

I travelled to you that day I was told you awaited me in the coffee shop (Sorcerer's Apprentice in the early 80s) A pagan paradise. Saturday mornings it was the in place to be

I entered you were sat surrounded as always by other walkers of the paths who could listen to you for hours, you saw me made a big fuss, making people I thought knew more than I move so I could be next to you. You embarrassed me by saying I had just completed a three-month penance something none of them could do. You were so proud of me.

Later when I began to teach others and brought my first students down to meet you enjoyed yourself telling them all the stupid things I did whilst learning magick's, then embarrassed me further by telling them I was an excellent teacher and they had chosen well

I never felt special, or great, I just did what came naturally but by then I had learnt humility

When I first cast a circle for you, I was scared you would think it was crap but you didn't you jumped inside saying don't shut me out you scolded me for saying something in Latin I could not translate and I learnt to translate

Those days seem so far away now, and I miss them I wonder about those who walk the paths these days now it is all diluted down stuff and not just a path in a dirt track with a few rocky groves.

I wonder if they will ever feel that special place, that dawn that never ends if they will ever know a teacher as great as I have

When they deride hierarchy, do they not know that the blind cannot lead the blind that wisdom does not come from books, self-denial, drugs, or alcohol that it comes from dammed hard work the way of the Wyrd is not a right it is a well-worn tool that can be used to shape the self in the good of humanity, that everything in the universe bows to something else

DEDICATED TO RBB MY TEACHER. /FRATOR. /

IN THE SERVICE OF LIGHT

SOROR ASHNA……….

He was 89 years young…

RBB died Christmas eve 2000…

Can you see em when they are dead?

In 1968 my beloved granddad died from bowel cancer very quickly, in those days they did not have the treatments we have today. He was such a lovely man simple working-class bloke of 5ft tall I choose to remember him standing at the garden gate smoking his pipe. He would lean on the gate and stop me as I was on the way to school, say where its thou going lass? I never went to school lass did not learn read till I was 18 to write came later on at the mill. He was the proud father of five 3 girls 2 boys my father James was one of them, but he called him Jim or jimmy. My father told me lots of tales about the things he got up to as a lad, they lived in west riding part of Yorkshire Keighley to be exact at 305 west lane in a 1930s semidetached house with 3 gardens.

The back garden being the largest it had a path down the middle for gran to hang out the washing. The old Anderson shelter my granddad had put in during the war was there it had the veg patch on top of it. We turned it into our den it had these camp beds an old stove with stuff to make tea. We had the tin plates cups to play with, the old lamp as well it was ace playing in here dad said it was not ace in the war having sleep in there all 7 cramped in like sardines in a can. There was the old outside loo had one of those pull chains with an oak topped seat a rug on the stone floor. The old coal shed at the bottom he kept gardening stuff there.

father said once he took his little brother to the flics, he took him into a horror movie his brother shits his pants. So, dad had to miss the film they had sneaked into. He said his mother brayed him. Another time his brother terry said hey cut open the flock mattress sew me inside; they will wonder where I went do it for a laugh. Dad did it he cut open the mattress his brother climbed inside, and my dad took his mums sewing stuff and sewed him up inside it. When his mum came to say good night, she asked where terry was no idea said dad. She looked everywhere for him then came back heard giggling undid the mattress told them off for ruining it. My dad said he had a particularly good childhood except when they were 8 his brother 6 years old, it was war time stuff was rationed his mum had bought Apricot jam in a catering tin from the black market. One morning he asked what was to eat his mum said jam & cake eat it or starve. My dad chose to go hungry. He hates apricots because of this jam He told us that many times in the war he had only dripping, and bread eat. I tried it with salt on it was nice. At school they asked the kids to put up their hands if they had not eaten today, his brother kicked his legs held down his hand. Saying mum would not want you say nought. The kids came back saying they had an egg with toasted soldiers. He said at playtime he beat his brother up.

When my granddad died my gran stopped taking care of herself, my gran was a plump lady with permed short curly hair she wore stockings and pretty dresses plus a wrap over pinafore but in her grief 43 years married and still in love with her Tom. So, my dad said I could go stay with her, so she had someone she loved to care for. I slept in my dads' room in his bed. It was so comfy I never wanted get up, but my gran was strict breakfast at 8am lunch at 12 tea at 4pm and supper at 9pm bed at 10pm.

She cooked good food; her breakfast was cornflakes with warm sterilised milk it made them taste so nice. Followed by toast and jam with Yorkshire tea. We always ate at the table it always had to have a cloth and napkins it was my job to set table, to dry up and put away. The house was an incredibly old design I think we best take you through it help you see it the way I do, we did not use the front door We used the back-door downside garden. As you step inside you see two wooden latched doors one either side of you one was the pantry, the other the walk-in coal shed it was awfully long and dark inside it Two bags coal looked lost inside here. This opens up into the kitchen with its table and chairs straight ahead to your right is the sink with the wooden drainer a red curtain hung covering the cleaning stuff under sink. A wooden work top ended that side. Gran had a twin tub washer against one wall near the bathroom. it was not really built to have a bathroom, but granddad had converted the old washhouse to a bathroom with a big deep bath with rounded brass taps that bath was so big it was ace soak in, the inside loo. I was so happy I did not have to go all the way to the bottom of the garden to pee. There was this old-fashioned cupboard with glass doors on a wall and one of those free-standing cupboards with a pull-down top after all it was the 60s. Her kitchen smelt of fresh baked bread and cakes she baked all the time. Grans moto was if it is not breaking do not fix it, if tha wants to summate tha earns money pay for it or tha goes without. She did not believe in credit, they had to manage on mill wages. We then enter the living room along the front wall was the windows above here the pelmet with my seven handmade dwarfs on it. Then the main wall with the fireplace in it made from old bricks, above here was pictures and the mirror next to this was the built-in cupboard with four draws below it, Gran kept her best crockery in here and her brandy. In that corner was my granddads chair, then the sideboard an old oak one with two cupboards and two draws. Gran would put the pipes and Baca in the draw. Grandad would say Clara what is tha done with it, I put it where it always is, I canst find it, then open tha bloody eyes. I used to giggle when this happened, I loved the Banter between them. Most of all Saturdays at 4pm the boxing was on Gran would get all excited she would shout at the TV say stop ballet dancing and hit him. It was lovely she only drank one brandy of a night in her milky drink. I loved her so much.

In the middle of the lounge was the wooden two-seater sofa, with another chair the same to the window side at the back of the room was another sideboard but here she kept all her sheets and towels. The floor had one large woollen rug that came to just after the sofa at the hearth was another wool rug. At night, my gran would pull the furniture away from the fire roll up her rug. She said it was in case coal fell out of hearth. This was her routine, she cleaned everyday her house was her pride and joy. The door to upstairs was in back wall. The stairs had one of those carpets that only did the middle of the stairs. They curved around at bottom and top. Upstairs was only three rooms 2 large one small. My father said when he was small him and his brother Terry had a ¾ bed in there with the draws that was all. His sisters all shared a room which Jean the eldest hated. Mum and dad had the biggest room. He said nothing had changed inside since he was a lad. The outside toilet was a brick-built building next to the shed. it had a mat on the floor and newspaper hung on string not toilet roll like the indoor one. Dad said when they were small, they had to make sure the newspapers went there, and they had to cut them up and put then inside the old metal breadbin. With the toilet being downstairs my gran would give me a bucket at night with a bit of pine disinfectant inside it. She taught me many things like making rag rugs from old coats. How to knit, sew, bake, cook meals. We had great fun. So, I had no need to go through the house at night. one night several months after living there my gran woke me in the middle of the night, she was flushed acting a bit scared and nervous she said Canst you see em when they are dead?

Maybe not all the time though

I will sleep here you go in my room for tonight

Ok I said yawning

Grans bedroom was huge it had this huge bed with a big bolster and four duck feather pillows with her name on the edges. It had this big eiderdown in pink and several blankets of cream wool. The sheets were cotton and always smelt good. I climbed into it and wriggled about stretching across the bed in a zig zag way, the room felt a lot colder than normal it was autumn, but the frosts had not come yet, so I could not get why I could see my breath. Along the side wall was the big oak wardrobe given her as a wedding gift. She kept her photos on the shelf in here along with her hats. A few minutes later, I saw the bottom part of the bed sink down, this was getting frightening like a person was sat there. I hid under the sheets, then the covers were peeled back at one side right alongside me the weight of a person was getting into the bed the pillow developed a head shape, yet I could not see anyone. It was really creeping me out. I had my feet outside the bed ready to run. But then the voice said

Hey lass move on up will you tha had all the bed

Clara lass come on I need some room at least lass shift thee arse over. Oh, Clara lass me feet are cold, shall we light fire tonight its bit nippy. Come on lass hold me I needs a hug love.

The voice I knew it was my granddad Tom

Grandad, I said is it you?

Oh, darling what's tha doing in here?

Where is my Clara?

In dads' room

Why?

I think you may have scared her

Oh, lass I was wanting a hug is all, I miss her so I told her I would not leave her I said I would wait for her. She kissed, me and said do not be a daft a path.

But granddad your dead, dost tha think I do not know that love.

Whispers of the Witch by NanyWytch

I can give you a hug if I can see thee, they did not let me come say goodbye when you died that day, I miss you too

We hugged all night as far as I know as I fell asleep in my granddad's arms that night but, in the morning, he was gone

I tried to tell my gran, but she would not listen to me. she said hey lass once they have gone that is it, you just get on with it best you can. come on eat the food and cheer up, she hugged me kissed my head saying I miss him too love. I tried again saying but he is here gran, do not be daft lass.

Many years later when I was 18 married and pregnant with my first child the Drs wanted me go hospital stay for a week's rest. We were staying there till our house was ready. I was packing the bag upstairs in grans room when a voice shouted my name. I thought it was Michael so shouted downstairs I am here what is up? He said nought love why? Puzzled I goes back to my job the voice came again shouting my name. I went downstairs convinced it was Mike. He was in the kitchen with gran helping cook lunch. I go back upstairs shaking my head thinking I have now lost it. Then the voice shouted right at the side of me, I turned around said what?

The voice did not sound familiar at all. He said you will be OK no need to worry love your having a girl she will be well as will you. You do need to rest so do not fret anymore. I said but how do you know, he said in spirit we know a lot.

I went downstairs to tell Mike and Gran about it, gran smiled saying do not be so daft lass.

Whispers of the Witch by NanyWytch

My Teacher the Magus Richard Bartle Bitelli

Whispers of the Witch by NanyWytch

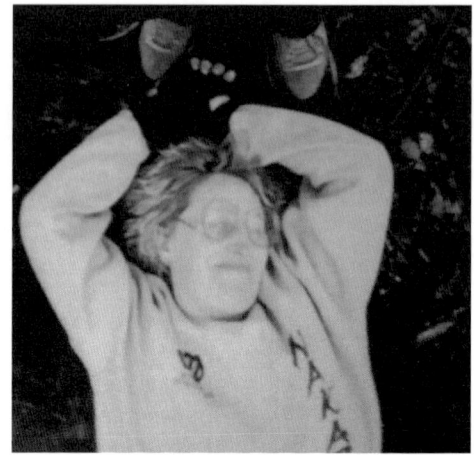

The war hero

Whispers of the Witch by NanyWytch

we had sort of adopted an old guy from over the road who had no family he would come over chat to my mum have Sunday lunch with us. We got to know him very well. He was a world war one veteran he his brother and best mate had signed up in 1913 to join army they lied about their age because they had lived in a horrible boy's school, their father had placed them there when their mother died and he couldn't mind two boys and go to work. In the war they were all ok till 1915 when they went over the tops together and they hit a mine as they ran Alf saw his brother and best mate blown to pieces in front of him. He got lots of shrapnel in his body and was knocked out, he woke up in a hospital with shell shock (PTSD) and all these small cuts where they had dug out the shell casing. He was sent home at 18 years old. He said he suffered very badly with shell shock kept on seeing his brother and best friend blown up, he said if there was a loud bang he would be on the floor. His flat was like going back to the 1890s he had a beautiful oak dresser in his lounge with 8 draws in it, he kept his shirts there and other clothing. It had a secret draw in which he kept his passports bank books some cash and his will plus insurance, He showed it to me asked me recall how to open it, I did easily he said not to forget. He used to go to town every day to a café to eat breakfast, the one in the bus station that is now closed down I would go with him sometimes and he would buy me a bacon sandwich and cuppa cha. One day he went the travel agents to book a holiday in Canada for one month. He said he was going to stay with his nephew his only living relative. That night I had this awful dream that the flight number he was going to be on would crash into these snow-covered mountains and no survivors were found. 333 passengers had died. I woke up sweating as I had watched the plane go down due to engine failure at 39,000 feet. I decided I didn't want Alf to die, you have to remember I was still a very young girl aged 9 I knew that if I moved his hat, he would miss the bus then train to Leeds then have catch a later flight, so on the day he was to travel I went over with the excuse of saying have a nice holiday give him a hug say I would miss him, but whilst he was brewing up, I moved his hat to the bedroom. When we had enjoyed our tea Alf said it was time to go but he could not see his hat, so he said have you seen where I put my hat? No, I said but I can help you look for it, yes, he said I need be on the 8am bus to get train and plane it was now 7,45am although the bus stop was just a few yards away I knew Alf couldn't run and walked slowly with his stick. He said I do not know I feel a bit sick really, I do maybe it is that I am going so far to see someone I have never met in my life. I got his hat, and we left the house but as we got to the path the bus had just gone, dam it said Alf we have 30 minutes to wait let us have another brew. We did but I made it this time I love being with him he reminded me of granddad in some ways and it was nice to learn about the war from someone who had been there he told me that someday you were treading up to your knees in mud that they were all scared and some pissed themselves before going over the top, that they had stay in those clothes as they couldn't change in a pit full of dead bodies and crap.

Alf got the 8.30am bus and he caught a later train from Leeds and got a later flight, all day I was waiting for the news at 6pm I sat down with dad to watch it and it said that a plane had crashed due to engine failure and there was very little chance of recovering anyone from these mountains, I said to dad Alf would have been on that plane Yes, he said but he isn't a few hours later we got a phone call saying Alf had arrived safely in Vancouver.

Often it doesn't work out this way, many times I have had these types of dreams but been unable to prevent the person from getting the bus or train you cannot just walk up to a stranger and say don't get the train it's going to crash, they wouldn't believe you and sometimes you just know you're not meant to. Alf became a very close friend of the family he had a picture of me at school in his wallet. When he fell one day, he could have been a Chelsea pensioner live in one of their places, but he said he did not want wear another uniform. Back then there was very little treatment for Shell shock, he suffered badly. The police arrived at my home when my first child was but a baby, asking if I knew Alf Murhall, I said of course they found me via my school tie. Alf had hurt his head badly and been transferred to an old peoples home in Bradford. My husband and I drove there to see him, the shock of what I saw will remain with me my whole life. Men like Alf who had served their country sharing one large dormitory. Wearing dirty soiled pants one man drank from the pics pot, claiming he was extremely thirsty. They put this woman in the room with us Alf said in a whisper you have to get me out of here. She took my pension book from me and my wallet and house keys, so I need help. We walked in the large gardens this woman following us all the time he was allowed no privacy at all. He said at night they are locked in that dormitory, I asked about clean clothes he said we have nothing none of us they take it off you here. We decided that Alf was coming home with us could have the spare room. The manager sat in his extremely plush office, he refused to give me Alf's property based on the fact we were not blood relatives. So, we simply called the police I said they were holding this man against his will, the officers who came spoke to Alf on his own, then said that a Dr must examine him to confirm he was of sound mind. Once this was done Alf came with us to our home. The fact his flat was only 5 minutes' walk from his own place helped him re settle. A few months later he wanted go home, so was permitted to. We sadly moved away to Blackpool several years passed by and we had a letter from relatives saying Alf had fallen and died, we were having a party, but I felt him close by me saying goodbye. His great nephew came from Canada sold everything not knowing about the secret draw. So, whoever bought it might have found it. But of course, it was too late. On remembrance days I think about him.

The picture in the hall.

Whispers of the Witch by NanyWytch

I attended a rather nice high school, if you were different you could be picked on by those lasses, who thought of themselves as the best of us. However mostly they were the ones who lost their knickers to a lad. So, I kept to just my mates, our little group of outcasts, it is a psychological need to want be with others like yourself, but finding another psychic, empath in the 60s was like looking for buttercups amongst daisies. The outcasts were 6 girls all of us 13, who for a variety of reasons did not quite fit the mould the mean girls had decided was the err mm Norm. Jane had been burnt over 60% of her body, Karen was the fat girl, Susan was the girl with orange skin, Lisa was the girl with no mummy, and Beverley was the posh kid coming into our high school which was anything but posh. I well I was that weird kid you know the quiet one knew stuff said little. We being prefects normally hung around in the hall hugging a radiator, this particular day was very normal except double maths had been swopped for double Religious education. Taught by nuns, on the wall right opposite our radiator was a framed picture of the Hay way by constable. I could not help it something about that picture really got to me. Today there was this musty sort of cloud above the cart. Maybe it was dust, but I just could not stop staring at it. Then I saw Beverley Colliers face appear, she said Ash tell them I are not going be in school Monday. There was this pile up on motorway Saturday afternoon our car was in the middle. We my family were all killed. Tell them I love them ok. I nodded after phasing out from the conversation. Margery hit me hey you we are asking what you got planned for later on. Oh, sorry I had to just well, hey you talk to us come on. I just came out with its Beverley is dead, she died in car crash on m6 Saturday. How do you know? She told me, hang on idiot if she is dead how is she tells you smoke signals. Your being weird again let us talk about something else are you still coming mine for tea. My mum says you could have a Saturday job at the hotel if your parents allow it. Yeah, am coming it is a yes to that too. Karen's parents ran a bed & breakfast on palatine Road. I stayed there sometimes, in summer her whole family slept down in the cellar. Wintertime they chose a room sleep in, so it was rather fun pick a room you had never slept in before.

It was time for mass again, I hated this part of the day it was always the same never ever changed a tiny bit. after the prayers and the priest waffling on they had chosen a hymn that always made me cry the old, rugged cross, it was my granddads favourite song. So, everyone is singing, and Lisa is holding me as tears stream down my face. It always happened after all he had not long been dead.

The head we called Marshmallow, because he was so soft on us all being girls, he had worked at this school when it was just boys. He said I have some news for year 3c would they remain behind after the others have left. What you think he wants? Oh well he might want tell you about Beverley being dead. For god's sake she is on holiday in Spain not dead. I said yeah, they were on holiday till Saturday when driving up M6 a lorry crashed into them she is very dead. Ash you are creeping me out, how you know this stuff? I reply spirits find me tell me shit. Wow I would like that you mean like gods angels come fly in leave you a note. Sticking out my tongue at Susan I say how do you know angels can write, you cannot. Oh, I forgot you cannot read either. Bitch I hate you, no you do not you love me because I am so cuddly and sweet. You are still a bitch though. Marshmallow said a girl in your class was involved in a car accident and will not be re-joining us on Monday. Sadly, Beverley collier died Saturday afternoon on the M6 in a multi car pileup. The family has requested that those girls she was close to are invited to attend the funeral this Friday you girls will attend with her teachers in full school uniform in the school bus. We will be leaving after lunch. We have counsellors available if you need to talk. Plus, Father John will lead a mass for her tomorrow morning. We all, piled out of the church, back into school, my mates said girl you are weird. You told us outside we made fun of you. Holy frap, you must have a hot wire to god. No way I am allergic. Being kids we just got on with it, parents think death is some big thing when actually its far easier if they talked about it. I do not think I would have been as upset about my granddad if they had let me see him to hug him goodbye. Spirits told me it was like waking up from a dream. You walk to somewhere else.

Sister Margaret was balling her head off, Father John was hugging her, she loved our Beverley because she said she was the Bonnie's brightest girl in our class.

Friday came it was a bit creepy as her family consisted of these not dead, in church I saw all of them even her baby brother. Beverley was sitting on top of her coffin dangling her feet offside. She did not look any different than normal except her leg was not right her foot was backwards. She had these marks on her. They could see me her brother said to me how can you see me if they cannot? I said not sure are you OK now. Sure, we are just dandy I am missing my mates though I wanted be in the rugby match Saturday. My mates will not know I are not coming they go to St Joseph's over the fence. Will you tell James and Gary I are not coming? I said I can try but do not think they let girls into St Joseph's. Yeah, he said maybe I should do it wake him up at night tell him. Yeah maybe, but we have this code if you can hang a pair of girl's pants on the flagpole they will know. You want me sneak into a boy boarding school with girl's gym knickers hang them on the flagpole why there. It is our code for something wrong cannot make it.

Phew Chris you are asking a good girl climb over there leave this weird message for your rugby team mates. You can do it I can help your I can get you into there because of the secret hole in our fence. I can fly them up to their, but I cannot hold em. They must be the navy-blue kind.

Jeez Chris when later on today before they bury me as no idea what happens to me then, do not suppose you know. He will no I do not. Our Beverley called you the weird kid. Said you were a bunch of outcasts the mean girls picked on. She wanted me leave a note in that Sharon's desk. A note what is it going say, that she will haunt her for pushing her head down loo.

I can put that in the desk for you, Beverley came said hey talk to me too, I said nobody else can see you only me do you ever wonder why Father Michael or Father John can't when they say they represent God on earth. If they cannot see you, can they see angels. Doubt it but who cares. I wanted hug Beverley, but she was all misty and see through.

We did hang those draws for Chris though we sneaked through the fence and tied them onto the flagpole pulled them up they looked great. On the Monday we were all asked how gym knickers from our school ended up in St josephs.

We were all told it was sinful to go into the boy's school, so we had remained secluded in our side to protect us from sinful ways

What kissing boys in the changing rooms oops sister Francis would go all red. Have you ever wondered why god needs all these women as his wives when they do not have babies like Mary whom was our goddess first, maybe god just likes singing nothing else because he only has Virgins? I often wondered had they ever been kissed at all because I know Father Michael had he had been married before being a priest. He was my favourite priest Father John was far too up his own bum to be nice to people he was just too pompous. Talked about that book as it were written by God himself which we all know is not the truth at all. Often I thought on if they only knew what the angels said to me it would really open their eyes, however maybe they do not want to see the truth for what it is.

By the time I was 14 years old I had been hiding in the library after school researching being different I simply needed to know what these things were I could do that others could not. Why was it like this. I never told the priests as they would say I was possessed by the devil, I did not believe in. Simply because my research said a pope invented him scare the peasants in the 14oos. You have to recall nobody could read nor write except church folk or kings. Well one day I opted take some books home, read in bed at night. I put my school bag and the books down on our dining room table. Mum said to get milk from shop as one of my brothers had drank it put empty bottle back. So off I goes to the shop not thinking about these books at all, because my father was still at work. When I came in my dad was ranting and raving about not having this devil worshipping crap inside his house. He grabbed the books was throwing them onto our fire, burning them after ripping them up. I laughed he said why is this funny come on let me into your sick joke. I said they were not mine they belong the school library. Why did thee not say so? Well, you were busy yelling and screaming you taught me its rude interrupt adults. Dammed idiot, I will have fork out for them now, yes I said giggling walking away. I never brought books home again my mum would say hush do not let your dad know ought about it love it is our secret you see mum & I had this telepathy thing we could have chats that nobody knew about.

Whispering Walls

Whispers of the Witch by NanyWytch

I was now married with two beautiful girls one aged two the other nine months it was 1979. Our home was mortgaged, and we were now two months behind with payments they decided to foreclose as we had no idea when we would be working again. So now we had fallen off that ladder slid down a big dark hole fast into homelessness. We had ended up in a hostel for the homeless which used to be the old workhouse with its for-boding buildings all the allure of a prison. The walls still had emblazed on them workhouse. Long cream coloured damp corridors, the wash house had sinks aligning the walls and a few washing machines in the middle with lines outside for the washing. Women sat crying taking Valium whilst snotty nosed children ran around without shoes in the yard. The place stank of damp and black mould crept up some walls like a dark black monster making its presence felt every day. having been there 4 months already my husband now had a new job fixing tyres where he had use of the works van, it made life easier when we weren't dependant on benefits my husband had never ever been without a job so when he was it hit him rather hard. On this day I had £10 till Friday it was Wednesday today we needed milk bread and wipes so I went the shop across the road was gazing at the magazines when without any warning nobody in sight one hits me right on the head, slips to the floor opening up on a page where a box sought of caught the light of the sun and shone out at you as if it were jumping from the page. I put it back saying to spirit not today I need these things. No, they said today throwing it at me again. I knew I could not afford spend £3 on paper. So, said no again to them walked outside stepped onto £10 nobody was about See they yelled in my ears. I walked back in bought it took it back with me later as the kids were in bed, I read the magazine the advert they kept lighting up for me. It was for occult contacts, So I sent the stamps and letter and thought nothing more of it. Dr said we needed to be moved to a no damp room, they claimed they had none but a few hours later they moved us to a better room where we even had our own bathroom and kitchen.

I bought new fresh bedding 2 new rugs and a few toys for them to play with, we got better being in this room where the windows opened. The social worker got them into nursery for me so I could spend time re organising the place making a bedroom for them we could close off as the council said we may be there another 6 months yet.

I dreamt about a house down a twisted lane with boards at the windows, elderberries, rowan and blackberries growing from the bushes lining this twisted lane. It looked so out of character as if it were stuck in times past, as I walked the lane there was no sounds of the road at all. A package arrived the very next day with a huge list of contacts. letters were sent to a box number they posted them onwards. So first I used my pendulum across a map picked three places Manchester, Dewsbury, North Shields. I had not a clue right then but later I would discover all these three were connected. Then I used the pendulum to pick 3 names for me a girl in a coven in Manchester called Marie, a Magician in Dewsbury, a high priestess in North Shields. Sent off my letters and thought nothing about it just like I had done with my runic spell asking the Gods help find us a home where I said I didn't care if it were in a field as long as it was a home where I could be free practice my magic's. A few weeks pass by when I get my first letter back it was from Marie in Manchester however this letter really got to me in an unexpected way. When I was last alive, I was a witch then with others we were all betrayed and then half drowned then hung from a bridge as witches. Her letter told me all about the coven she was in, its members even where they met up the details were such had I wanted to harm them I was armed with all the information I needed. I felt awful I was scared upset and angry that this girl would behave this way. That what she was doing was a betrayal of her brothers and sisters what I did know is that there was no information readily available to find those witches, who were in covens or indeed how to get into one if you like me wanted to learn. My next letter came from the Magician he told me all about his family and that he had been working magic's for over 40 years he asked if I would visit him and his family once, we knew each other better he gave me the house phone number said If I had any problems   I did I ring him we talked for over a hour this was when he told me that he knew the High Priest and Priestess who had taught the High Priest of that coven in Manchester the web grew, what were the gods up to I asked him He said well the Gods do not like oaths taken before them broken. So, they are using you as the messenger. the Gods want you to learn so if you are the messenger it could solve both issues, but it makes me sound like the bad guy here, no way he said it brings the news to them that she cannot be trusted nothing bad about you. So, I said what am I to do and what if she gets killed, he calmed me down said no that will not happen I can vouch for that. He said he would contact the people for me but if I got a letter from the priestess, I ought to tell her how worried I am why. I did get a letter from the priestess who advised me to stop all communication with the girl right away or I could get tarnished before I even started on the path properly. I knew that RBB was going to talk to them as well about me. He told me that long ago when covens needed sacrifices of the oak king at the end of summer, He had voluntary walked off a cliff during the ritual. Now he was forever linked to them. No matter that this life he walked a totally different path where Isis was his goddess.

I have to say I fretted over this girl terribly due to my past experiences and the fact we were betrayed I guess it upset me to my very core nature.

Whispers of the Witch by NanyWytch

On the 16th April 1980, the woman came from the office to say you have a call in the office from housing, they had a house for me to see. I had collected the keys and go see it. The girls were at nursery so it was not an issue except I needed call them and ask can my husband collect them today at 5.30pm they said of course love. I got in a taxi set off to find the place. 190 Squires Gate Lane East we drove up Squire's Gate Lane several times could not find side road that said it was squires gate lane east. We went to the post office the lady said yes love beyond the 16th century cottage down the lane. I told my burly rugby player driver around 40 years old huge man fit not fat. He pulls a face looks rather scared at me says lady I am not taking thee down that lane bad shit happened down there. I thought how silly he was being scared of things he had heard in the pub being a witch, I did not care if it had monsters, under the bed I was going down here to find this house. I step foot onto this lane with its twists and turns I am thinking how peaceful it is here, birds chirping the sound of running water gurgling across rocks. I moved tree branches and there it was this small stream working its way down the hill over the rocks then vanishing underground part way down. The wild mint grew from its banks other herbs could be seen scattered about the hedges. The weird thing was this was so like my dream as there were elderberries hanging from last year plus blackberries, rowan and many herbs clinging to the edges of this dirt track. The silence was rather eerie as the noise from the road abated, I saw a roofless white house on the left-hand side so I went to look at it   the entire roof was on the floor it covered carpets and furnishings the walls were covered in oil the tank on the floor amongst the rafters. Guess the owner liked the splash and puddle effect décor. the owner in his folly had placed an oil tank in his loft and filled it goodbye roof and house. an owl sat in what was the rafters watching me silently.   I turned to the right walked down some more to the fork in the old cart track for that is what it was the ruts had to be from years of carts or a carriage maybe. Seeing a rusty old farm type gate swinging off one hinge I pull it open to venture inside guessing this must be the place. I stopped mouth open not only was there a house, a huge house, but a stable several outbuildings even greenhouses a bit overgrown but what a surprise. I did wonder why it was only £10 a week rent. It seemed rather large for the money. But as they say beggars cannot choosers be, I carried on viewing the stables first it had stabling for two horses, room for a trap or cart, upstairs a bale of hay sat all alone housing for the mice now.

I walked towards the doubled fronted old house around the back to the conservatory, not the modern type that old-style part brick part glass like Victorians built. one ledge for plants all the way around. Through here was the back door, a small oak door that was rather hard to push open, I came to a large square shaped room with a big fireplace and wood burner the old pottery sink with wooden drainer, plus the old table with the middle almost scrubbed out was the only things here. I did not have much light as there were boards at the windows, I did have a torch I had been given at the housing office as the man explained about the boards. I stepped through the next small oak door and was renderly impressed at the size of the room before me wow!

The panelling itself looked old as well as the wooden floors with wide planks of oak were very old indeed, the fireplace here was very big higher than myself at 5' 4" I was very intrigued about this place, I took a door on my right which led to a corridor type place that didn't go anywhere just abruptly ended. it had a branch to the right that ended in a very antique looking door so short even I would stoop but it was nailed shut.

the voices began who is she? what does she want? she can hear us, I listened laughed said its rude to not introduce yourselves. as I went to the large stairwell in the hall, I caught a glimpse of a boy around 8 years old torn collarless shirt, trousers just below the knee no shoes no socks rough cut hair, who turned around said I am Jack by the way another voice a girl said shhhhhhhhh Going up the oak stairs with the angel picture window catching the sunlight so rainbows shone down the hallway. I go into the biggest room of all it goes from the front of the house to the back one window each side picture windows just like the one at top of the stairs   one had a knight on a horse with a cross on him. The other was again an angel, in here there was a broken record player. I knew there was no power on, yet it played run rabbit run song I picked up the wire no plug I smiled funny I said, Then the door banged shut loudly I turned around, no handle on this side. Aww I said well first your rude now your being petty open the dam door or I will. It opened very slowly I heard footsteps running away.

The next room was on my left up a couple of steps this had an oak door just like the others hard to open the room was large I guess this could be the master bedroom from its size the fireplace here was just like the one downstairs. A door to my left caught my eye. I walked inside, a full-sized window like the others yet this room ended a few feet in like those downstairs, something was not making sense here, it was like part of the house was missing. Going back to the hall I enter the back bedroom large again, but this had this creepy rickety small staircase going up to the attic. Remember I only had a torch and not much light as all windows were boarded up. I climb the stairs to find a room the size of half the house filled with chests, furnishing left behind at some time in the past. I wandered in to find a desk chair, sideboard, bookcases, huge set of draws, dolls pram, dolls house with wooden furniture. And a few chests filled full of clothing and books.

I saw the time and thought I had to go I had not realised how long I had been there. It was now 1.30pm I needed get to the main road to go across to the garage phone a taxi. So much easier these days with mobiles. managed to get to my appointment with minutes to spare the man said well as your homeless we give you one property to go see and expect you to take it, I said yes please. He said they would give us a grant of £500 start us off with things we needed. They would put the power back on remove the boards and turn on the phone us being quiet away from the main road. I call my husband at work tell him we have a house and to pick up the girls for me today He was so excited he sounded like a little boy at Christmas mind you I was on a high too Mike wanted to move out of that place today when he came home, he said we can buy some food sleep on the double airbed I have and light the fire I said we needed candles or torches. I packed up what we had in less than an hour and sat there thinking about that house it was so odd. Those voices had sounded like children, but I only glimpsed the boy. We moved into the place that night turning off the road into the lane which was very bumpy indeed as we drove down it, I was the navigator, so Mike said. He noticed it too that sort of odd feeling like time had stopped still here. We lit the fire and made our bed in the lounge settled the girls down after feeding them I had bought a trifle we even gave some to the baby it so pitch-black outside and you could only here the owl which I discovered lived in the barn. to be honest the house had this darkness it did not have during the day the type that crept into your very soul. It was silent though a bit too silent really. But with the fire burning and a bed set up on the floor for us all sleep in we enjoyed that feeling of having somewhere to call home. Over the next few months, we built ourselves a nice home using furnishing from the attic as well as buying new carpets and blinds. I set up a temple in the front lounge to my goddess Diana. Life went on I did not hear anything more from those spirits for a while not until my 3-year-old was sat on the stairs singing in French. I said Tanith where did you learn that song? The girl with the metal on her legs, she plays with me here. Her name is Susanna.   Tanith come with me to the kitchen let us get you that drink we can have it in there I asked her when does this girl come to play, she said night times mostly, she comes to the room upstairs, she plays with the dolly house. My dolls and talks to me she likes my raggedy Anny. Ok   tell me about her what does she look like? she wears this long dress nearly down to her ankles, with a piny over the top, has metal things on her legs. she cannot walk properly only very slowly. Her hair is dark with these funny curls in them, she is 7 years old and knows French and Latin she said she can teach me. Mummy she says she does not like you because you spoilt her game. What did you play? She likes to play hide and clap, but she is much better at hiding than me I can never find her up there in the attic its where she hides from him. Who I say? her daddy of course he is horrible he wants to kill her because her legs do not work, her mummy just cries all the time because the daddy is mean. It seemed my daughter knew a lot more than I did about the house's past. I guess the little girl had made a friend with my daughter, this did worry me as we knew nothing about this ghostly girl. The girls had the long, big room on the left of the hallway we had added new handles and a safety gate as Morgan was now a year old and walking. We took the Master bedroom of course and turned the other room into a guest room. We added a door from the stables to the weird staircase to the attic it was the old latch type door. We had cleared the grass and created bale fires on the big lawn with an outdoor altar Were had found the slate base of a pool table in the barn, so we built a frame for this it became our outside ritual space. We built a fire pit near the bale fires. It was my favourite garden. The girls still had plenty of space. We invited some friends to the Beltane festival and had a party where the girls hid, and the boys had to find them then they could do whatever they wished till midnight; one condition was nobody went upstairs in the house. My girls were sleeping there. RBB came too as well as many others I had met since becoming a witch myself. Being a witch before I had carried over many powers from my past one of them was bi- location another was the ability to hide amongst nature. During the game I had hid right near the front door in the small mature garden at the front I had put my arms around a tree and said please do not let them find me. The tree had listened and cast its shelter over me they even stood right on my toes and did not see me. I heard them saying we cannot find Ashna we have no idea where she is RBB looked worried, so I stepped out from the tree. You were there the whole time Yes you stepped on my feet as you were talking but you could not see me Well No we could not I laughed said it is just magic's. Months pass then suddenly one night it's all quiet, girls asleep I was dozing on the chair when I heard strange sounds coming from the room off the hall, I open the door to see a woman running down there in her long nightdress with a man chasing her they vanished through the walls where the room stopped. I walked back to the sofa said to mike did you see that. Nope he said was reading see what. No matter I say let us go bed. Soon after this thing went a lot worse all of a sudden. We were all sitting in the lounge one day my brother and sister were visiting my brother was a mental and physical medium and incredibly good at it too he saw spirits too. A mental medium can be used by spirits to speak through called direct voice. Whilst a physical medium can be used by spirits to walk through so they can be present in our time. Both can be dangerous without control. All of a sudden, the back door flew open and then the windows all opened and shut banging then all the doors upstairs were banging windows opening and shutting all at once. The kids took no notice they were far too engrossed in the cartoons. This banging and clattering went on for over five minutes a hurricane gale was blowing right through the whole house. I just stood there in the lounge and shouted enough now, or I get to play my game do you hear me. It went quiet again as suddenly as it had begun. This happened once a month now we were getting used to it every dark moon that came around it happened.

Whispers of the Witch by NanyWytch

One day the girls at nursery mike at work, I was alone in the house. I had let the dogs out shut the gates locked them, told the dogs go play. I started to clean house I began with girl's room stripping beds to put clean bedding on them, best get it done whilst have the time. As I walked into my room, I heard the front door open, then a child's voice sounded like Tanith. Which I knew it could not be as she was at nursery with her sister. It shouted in a kind of playful voice come and find me? I walked out of my room after making our bed, the girls room door was now open, so I go inside the toys were piled up high again. Then I heard giggling and the voice said come and find me? I followed the sound she was in the spare room jumping on the bed shouting in French bonjour madam assay vou. Morning Madam please sit down. I said what game is this then? Oh, I was bored the girls are gone where do they go? To nursery! Oh, I do not know that word what is nursery? It is a school for smaller children. I never went to a school my big brother did he stayed away a long time. So how did you learn Latin & French? My Father employed a governess for me, but he did not like me, he never wanted to see me. I was not supposed come down from the attic rooms they were my rooms. They did not let me go outside your girls go outside all the time, yes, they do but you do not go with them no the dogs do yes that black one chases me when I am in the field. You can see us, but others do not see us. Why? No idea maybe they are not tuned into the vibrations like we are. Tell me what happened to you? I do not know all I know is my father came with a servant put a cloth over my face I fell asleep. When I woke up it was all very different because I could run. Oh, your legs yes, the callipers have you always had them yes, my servant put them on after dressing me. So how long have you been here? A very long time, I guess. What happened to the people before me.? She laughs oh they ran away in the night. Guess they were afraid. Well, you do some pretty shitty things really. Me she yells you scare me! Rubbish I said you sulk is all. She laughs runs off I see her in the far field from bathroom window the dogs chasing her.

Strange fact was they never touched my temple room ever never opened that door not once nor its windows I did wonder why just that room was excluded from the games they played. Maybe it was the Gods protecting it . All summer it had just been this child who cried on the stairs at night but when you went to her, she backed off into the wall. We would see her running along the garden the dog hot on her heels carrying Tanith's raggy Annie. The salt and pepper would end up in the bath whilst the shampoo would be in the cupboard downstairs, small things moved about or vanished. Then turned up on the carpet or in the stable's months later. We met the man at the top farm, he was called Sid told us that his family had been on this land since the 1600s that they lived in the same cottage he lived in, he always had his shot gun slung over his arm sometimes we would hear him shouting I will get you don't you worry, He said nobody had lived in the house for 7 years aforeus, that the family afore had all but vanished one night. He asked if I had seen it, I said the child you mean, no he said the creature the one that protected the land it came back every autumn. I said well some odd things started to happen a few weeks back if that is what you mean. Lass he said you be careful down there this land does not like many folks it picks and chooses for itself. We know you are of the way too, let me show you the path we use to our secret meeting place they want to meet thee this full moon. We will come for thee. The full moon came, and we walked through our field with the neighbours took a fence panel out of our field and then followed a rough track to the next farm. It was nice to meet some other witches who were all family they talked to us for most of the night after the ritual I met Gary from the next farm after this he grew fruit asked what I might grow I said I have planted a lot of veg out there so we will have fresh food, they told me around these parts we all barter with one another has meat you can buy Half a Lamb or a full one, you ought arrange to barter with him we are all pagans around here. So, it looked like the Gods had placed me smack bang in the middle of many others to help me grow. One night not long after I heard children running about upstairs, I thought the girls were out of bed it was late. So, going upstairs I find the bath full of water taps running and a girl in the bath I empty the bath she was gone. They ran into my children's room toys were piled up in this huge tower with the Lego at the bottom the pram on top how it balanced I do not know but I was a bit worried about it crashing down onto Tanith's bed. I said put it all back if you ever harm my girl's I turn into your worst nightmare. Do you understand they ran off laughing then it went quiet again I lifted the pram down and moved things? These towers became the way they announced their presence here. It may be the chairs in the kitchen on top of the table all Higgledy Piggly. Or the books from the shelves or the toys it did irritate me some but most of the time I laughed saying not again put it back sometimes they would other times they just ran off but as it got more frequent, I was getting annoyed more especially when we had been out all day come back and the lounge furniture was in a pile. It seemed they were testing me how far did they need to go before I reacted in a negate manner. Did these energies feed them or was being positive the correct move?

Things would go normal for three months at a time after a clash with me winter was the worst the behaviour changed along with the opening and closing of windows and doors the whole atmosphere had gone very dark and oppressive. Things were happening every day. One night in November I heard my children screaming when I got there the toys were in that pile, they were both crying Tanith said I don't want to play with her anymore Mummy she has gone mean to me, she jumps on my bed to wake me up, steals my quilt, she is bad to me mummy calls me names and stuff make her stop mummy. Morgan just cried wanted sleep in my room I said just for tonight both girls ran into my room. I sealed the door and windows to prevent the spirits entering the girl stood in the hall staring at me, I said yes you can look at me but I said you were not to harm my girls tonight is too far I am going to stop you. She looked at me, all the doors banged most of the night guess she did not like it

I sealed my children's room taught Tanith how to do this and how to cast around her bed and sisters' bed. Again, we had peace.

Authors note.

Whispers of the Witch by NanyWytch

In the Saxon chronicle the land is described as rich arable land in Saxon strip farming method. with 20 tied cottages. In 1176 Merton village belonged to the Earl of Toasty's prior to this the Peveral family own the land. They lost it to the bastard count of Mortae.

By 1790 the village was a manorial land housing the justice of the peace. The nearest Catholic Church was then in Lytham the nearest Anglican Church was in Bishop ham.

Today the house, outbuilding, green houses are all gone on it are a selection of houses and the cart track is now part of the M55.

I often wonder whom got the anger of the guardian, how do the witches get to their place of worship now the land is gone. However, Geoff's farm still exists as does Sid's old cottage. I have to say I miss the place a lot. They intended it as temporary housing as they were already building the road. We did a working they ran out of money. So, we had a few more years.

Whispers of the Witch by NanyWytch

Stuff a nonsense

Not long after moving into the house we had a letter saying that we owed a bill for power. How could we owe them money we had been in a hostel for 9 months? We had not been in this house ¼ of the wheel yet. I called them some very rude person told me they were coming to turn off the power at the house. I had said we had just moved here this man was just not in a listening frame of mind. So, I decided I would stop this myself as we did not owe this firm money our electric was not by them.

On our temple room door, a sign read

This is an active occult shrine outside footwear is forbidden as are outdoor clothing.

Please never enter without the consent of the priestess the room is guarded by the unnatural.

We warn only the once.

My children said that a man with a big sword lives in there. I said yes so you do not go inside.

A man arrived from the company, he got out of his van was chased into the hedges by the dogs. I wondered why he had got out when on our gate a sign said

Do not get out of your vehicle if the dogs are loose. Beep your horn.

Whispers of the Witch by NanyWytch

The girls ran to us mummy the dogs are going to eat the odd man. I looked out the window there at the far end of the stables and outbuildings were the hedge dividing our land from Sid's land, this man was as far back into that hedge as he could get the dogs were inches away snarling at him teeth bared. I said to Mike shall we rescue him? No let him squirm a bit, let us have a coffee. So, we did we sat down knowing he was quite safe inside the hedge unless Oscar the stallion was out in the next field.

We walked outside called the dogs giving them treats for doing their jobs. Putting them inside the house. Walking towards him I said why are you on my land? I am from the electric company to cut the power here. Why did you get out of the car? Can you not read? Yes, but I saw the dogs rolling around on the ground with those small children even the tiny one. Well I said to those dogs they are part of the pack they protect. Hence, they chased you. Now are you coming inside as you need remove the coat and boots, we do not permit them inside the front of the house dirt from the fields.

Oh yes, he said I escort him through the front door leave him there taking off boots. I say I need get the keys unlock the door so walk away. Prior to him arriving I had been inside invoked the gods lit the fires burnt incense opened the dark mirror. Told them the intention afoot today that I needed justice, this was the day I had invoked a demon called Baphomet.

We had no bulbs in the light fitting instead a metal candle holder for 10 candles hung there. The windows were blacked out too.

The girls came to where this man was, they said to him you have to be quiet in there or you could wake him up the man with the sword he gets people cuts them all up. I said to go play but mummy he cannot wake up the warrior man can he. I said no he will be quiet.

The man had obviously read the sign he had been nearly eaten by dogs told there is something in the room he must not wake up. So, he was already nervous to say the least. After all he was just a workman not the man ordering the job.

Leading him inside he gazed about and then said is there no lights in here. Of course, not we use candles here. But the meter is right in that corner yes I said over their I do not know if I can see in the light. I said we have a torch for that. The meter was 10ft in the air, and he needed a ladder to get to it. We got him one, he started to climb it then swore I said shhhhhhhhh no profane language please I saw his legs shaking did not want him to fall off the ladder so offered hold it. Poor man said under the circumstances I do not think this appropriate. I think I ought to leave now. He rushed from the house across the gravel path outside the barn to his van fumbling with his boots. I walked the quicker way to him said now when you get back there. Sitting in the canteen you will say nothing about what you saw inside my house. I will know if you go blabbing to others and it will not be safe for you do you understand me. Yes, Ma'am he said but I will give the boss your letter.

Good day young man.

The bill vanished nothing was ever heard again about the matter, odd as to how pressing the man had been on the phone. I did feel for that workman though.

But are not children a blessing in disguise saying things that are not prompted.

We held a Housewarming party that very same night; many people were invited some were Christians. We had made a drink called witches brew in the huge cauldron. It was a very potent herbal drink. We will not say which herbs were in it but let us just say people were very relaxed and wanted more of it. When my sister saw it, she said why are there tea leaves in that drink. I said they are herbs dear you can eat them. Oh, will try it, she kept coming back for more. Our party was a great success but in the morning the girls had got up early watch cartoons everyone else sleeping. People had left drinks in glasses around the room, my girls decided to drink these bits. They fell asleep on the rug before the hearth when we came down, we realised they were drunk and stoned. We laid them on the sofa sleep it off. They had a habit of stealing my sugar cubes, apples give to Oscar the stallion who was so lovely he could jump the fence and was often found in our field munching the uncut grass. My girls just loved him he loved eating the apples but the farmer over the way did not much care for Oscars habits as he jumped his fences get to the mares, he mated all of them in one afternoon. The farmer come ranting to Sid about his mares all being pregnant Sid said well to be fair Harry he is a prime stallion I gets paid well for his seed in a mare. So, I will have two foals you keep three how is that for fair. That dammed horse better not be in my fields again or I will shoot him, Sid lost it, saying do not threaten to kill, my stallion you are getting 5 foals out of this I ask for just the 2 if not them I will have to invoice you for the mating with my pure-bred stallion 5 times.

Harry walked off tutting to himself, returning the next day with papers agreeing the deal.

Sid was a keen farmer his fields were never empty long, he taught me about the old ways of strip farming to get more yield.

Sowen

Roman catholic schools are very weird, being different is not really permitted here but I was a pagan not a catholic they were paid to take in some children from other beliefs. Mummy said do not use your magick in school, but sometimes its needed example getting bullied by a year 6 when your year 1 is not funny he was 10 I was only 4. Mummy said hit him back he is only picking on small kids because he is bigger but push him or kick him, he will stop. Bullies exist everywhere in life my love you need to learn how to deal with this.

He was stealing my lunch and really beating me up I had bruises from this but like my parents said I had to stop him, So I decided to use my magick this time. When I saw the boy coming towards me the very next day, I waited a bit then I moved to near the muddy puddle then I thought go on piggy fall in the mud you ought to be rolling in it piggy. As he reached out, I said =fall piggy. He did right into the mud, so I pushed his face into it with my foot. When he lifted his face up, I said if you try pick on me again, I will put worms in your lunch box boy. Go away.

He cried and got into trouble for being covered in mud it was great I felt good about this.

When I told my mummy back at home, she said

Tanith did you push him?

No mummy my hands were in my pockets the whole time.

Tanith, I did not ask where your hands were doing you push him

only a tiny bit I suppose we are allowed defend ourselves our laws say so she just smiled at me said go on play she was laughing guess she thought it was ok this time.,

Whispers of the Witch by NanyWytch

It was going to be Samhain pronounced Sowen, I loved this sabot best of all it is our its new year as well as ancestor's day. We decorate the place with pumpkin lanterns pinecones and fairy lights. We have a cauldron of apples in water. We have fireworks and great food mother baked for us. We do not do trick or treat as its not part of our belief system. We do dress up and have fun though. But we place pictures on our ancestor table for those that have left this realm to welcome them home we place food and wine next to them so they can enjoy family again.

The trees were almost bare the weather crispy, I would kick the leaves up our lane all the way to the top I loved that feeling running through my body of nature's breath spreading its wings into the leaves. The very transformation of the leaves with the vibrancy of colour was what made it my favourite time. but a long time ago this was when animals who would not survive the winter were culled and made into salted meat for the winter stores. To feed the villagers. Many would die at winter because back then they had no shops like we do.

Today at school our teacher said we were to paint two pictures and make a card to take home as it was Halloween soon, we were going to decorate the classroom too. So, I thought great fun in school art today nice one. However, as I started to paint my mummy with her cauldron and broom my teacher said Tanith, we are not painting mummy today we are painting witches. Well, I did not understand my mummy is a witch so why cannot I paint her. So, I looked at the other children's pictures and I was absolutely shocked one painted a woman in rags flying on a broom with a green face and big spots. Another painted a green spotty witch with a huge nose eating a baby and another painted a red devil with a pitchfork killing things. I never knew this is what they thought we looked like. To you this might seem not an issue but to me having been brought up inside a witch family it was tragic mother never told me they believed us to look this way and eat babies is this what church taught them? Any way what good is a witch who cannot clean her own skin or make herbal tinctures to get rid of spots. Wear nice clothes and feed her family. As for a green witch may be, they watched far too many cartoons.

Mummy would say we do not eat children these days as the fatty bits stick in your teeth, our broom does not fly it ran out of axle juice. So, it is to clean bad energies from our home. If you can make it fly go ahead. She did not turn people into frogs either but today I wished she would just turn the teacher into a big juicy one for our crows eat. In our beliefs we are taught everything comes from nature and to respect even the smallest bugs they all have a job to do. In fact, I had a pet spider called Fred who lived in the barn with his family he was married to Harriet and protected from the owl by me.

One day in the same week the nuns told us the story of Moses and going up a mountain to see god who gave him rules written on big stones. They did not tell you how one man carried them down that mountain as big as they were plus, he was nearly 200 years old by then. How they didn't explain in one of the rules it said Do not kill but, on the news, they were killing people so I asked is god not cross with them for killing people the nuns said I was being silly now why would he get cross? I said because they broke his rules. No child he never gets cross at all. But you see the angels said he could be very mean and selfish, and, in their book, it says he is jealous and selfish. Anyway, I think it's very rude not to turn up on a Sunday when you are meant to be their God after all you said you wanted them pray to you So are you sitting down on the job or did you always take the day off.

I had discovered I could move things without touching them I had not told mummy yet as did not know if it worked all the time. We were going to a psychic fayre in London and were on the train I was bored of colouring or reading I really wanted my sweets but was behaving like a brat. Mum gave me that look all mothers have them it means you are treading on thin ice stop right now or I will get you. At the very next station two nuns got onto the train they sat next to us we had the window seats opposite each other the table in between mother put my coke on her side of the table knowing I couldn't reach she said and the magick words are looking at me directly. I slumped back in my chair sulking then decided I was having that coke, so I wiggled my little fingers and said come to me come to me it started to slide across the table getting quicker the closer to me it got. Mother grabbed it said do it again, so I did it moved quicker this time. Mother grabbed it again said again. By this time, the nuns were crossing themselves saying holy Mary mother of god pray for us sinners now and at the hour of our death Holy Mary mother of god and the rest. They looked so afraid of this so I carried on it got faster the more I did it, now they were saying Lord have mercy Christ have mercy I wasn't bothered I knew all these prayers from school so mimicked them by saying the words as I dragged the coke over the table. I thought it funny that they thought this was evil and the devils work because that is what they were saying asking their god to protect them from this devil a creature one of their own popes created in 1464 to blame all the abuses they did onto. I sat back exhausted mother said sometimes it far easier to just take hold of something love. Yeah, but this was more fun I was sure of it. As soon as we came to another station the nuns moved seats after all the devil had invaded a 4-year-old child had he not the truth, but they never want to truth come out do they. After all we all know they stole most of their bible book from the Hebrews. They stole the bread and wine from the pagans and other stuff from other beliefs like Muslims. Yet the Jews, Muslims and Christians worship the very same God. After all they came from the same part of the east. It is a good story, but he always dies in the end and every year they do it all over again like let us celebrate the killing of our god's child I just did not get it but then I was only 4 years old. Yet I did like seeing nuns' squirm.

The Sealed letter

Whispers of the Witch by NanyWytch

I had received a letter bearing a read seal, addressed only to me. I opened this with my husband it said it was from the coven high priest and that he would like to meet me to discuss this letter from one of his conveners. I phoned the number agreed to a meeting the following week. making sure it was not a day he would be busy with the coven.

I met him at the railway station café he wore black and a silver pentagram on his sweater he looked like an intelligent well-turned-out gentleman. We sat and chatted, but it was constrained we did not talk about witchcraft as it was a public space, we had to be careful. I suggested we went to the house. We had these weird rules that if the dogs did not like you, you stayed outside. We had whisky and cross German shepherd with long hair he was our guard dog, but still very much family. Then we had another German shepherd dog too called Xavier, these dogs were rescue dogs and were now very much part of our home. I could say to them watch the girls they would all go play in the field I knew they were safe when with the dogs. One day the girls had wandered into the fields with the dogs whilst I was planting. One dog came back barking at me I followed him Morgan was half down a rabbit hole whiskey held her by her neck Xavier had tried dig her out. These dogs were wonderful guardians.

At the house he came into our lounge we did not allow shoes inside the rooms as it brought in contamination from outside. We chatted for hours about craft things then he asked about the letter, I let him read it his face said everything, I took the letter back. He asked could he keep it to which I said no its mine. He said he would need it to prove it was what it was betrayal of the craft. I was adamant I was keeping this letter I told him it worried me about what may happen to her, I said I was a witch before our whole coven had been betrayed by a stable hand we were half drowned then hung from the bridge. They killed the boy, so he did not get his gold coin. That boy was my brother in this life.

He asked me what I wanted most of all, I replied well let us see I want in so I can see what happens these days. I knew he had spoken to his elders and they to their own I knew I had been spoken about as I had met them all by now.

He said ok then Lammas will have to be the time but before then I needed to meet with him again to learn the ways initiated In, I agreed we parted as friends I had agreed that once I was initiated, I would hand over the letter so they could deal with the situation.

I knew they were all connected it always bothered me how on that day I used my pendulum that it had picked these people but then I believed the Gods decided for me what was best for me.

Lammas came very quickly, and I was incredibly nervous, when I arrived it was almost 7pm the people in the room I had never met before two blokes said I was the sacrifice for tonight. They left me all alone in the room wearing only a dressing gown, when someone came to the room I couldn't see their faces they wore robes and masks they bound me and blindfolded me and walked me into the ritual it took quite a while I had felt hot and cold been kissed and washed and blessed I had chosen my name as Circe, then it was light and they were all hugging me it was a nice welcome into the coven, the high priest and priestess called me into the room I gave them the letter when the high priestess read the letter she sighed on the bed saying well its best your with us then she explained to me that the 3rd levels will go into the room discuss the matter and then we would be allowed back into the room to not worry about this it's all over now, tonight it ends well for the coven.

Whispers of the Witch by NanyWytch

We were all socialising in the room when half of the members vanished the others said what's going on, I said no idea I had been told not to say a word, when we were allowed in, I was to stand next to John one of the 3rd levels Marie was just amongst the others in the circle, the high priest spoke about betrayal being something that was the worst crime a witch could do to her coven, he explained that in the past witches had been hunted and killed for less. He then called me to come to the middle handing me the; letter, he said Circe read it out please. I read it out one by one the conveners were looking terribly upset, I gave the letter back. he called Marie to the middle asking if she wrote this letter, she admitted she had done it. Months ago, maybe 5 months ago when she was very new to the coven and extremely excited about being in it. She was asked did she understand the gravity of what she had done. she admitted breaking the rules but declared she had no malice towards them. Everyone had a vote they had to put it into the bowl on the altar whilst she was outside the circle then they discussed how to proceed they took the envelope contained her hair and nails they had taken at her initiation and burnt them in the incense brazier. Then when she came back, she was told she was expelled from the coven that no convener would help her she was to leave now taking just what she came with. She cried begging them to reconsider I tried to say something, but Geoff put his fingers over my mouth whispering No keep silent you are a sister now. I am to help you learn as quickly as possible so you can do a gate. He explained that not all those present were of this coven some were of the elder's coven where they were taught.

I learnt very quickly, and my own powers grew fast as well I became 2nd; level in a few months by the following year I was heading towards my 3rd level. I attended coven every full moon and sabots. I went to see RBB as well for whole weekends so was learning not only Witchcraft but high magic's too.

Their all pagans here

Whispers of the Witch by NanyWytch

The church is a funny place, the priest asked me to procure some strawberries for the children. I asked why he could not go to Geoff himself he replied You must understand they are all pagans there I cannot be seen to associate with them

I said would do it for the children not for him as no I did not understand why he felt such fear of them. He sorts of waved his arms about almost red in the face They are all pagans you must grasp they well they worship the devil. I looked at him saying now that is a crock of shit.

I decided to take the back path our secret way why should I let the priest see me go. we never did allow them to know much at all twas better they made up what they knew. After all we had no devil to blame for our own errors of judgement. Arriving at Geoff I told him why I was here he went into a blue rage, he spat on the floor swore and profaned more than I had ever heard before. He said he would not smear his hands with the priest's gold it was tainted blood money smeared with the deaths of his family tortured and murdered by them.

The fruits of this land are grown by pagan hands with pagan toil blessed by our goddess he would not deprive children of their sweet taste. But he hoped the priest choked on his portion. I took them back to the priest dropping his coins on his desk, I said they would not take your gold they said it was smeared with the blood of their kin.

He said Oh god in heaven protect me from these pagans who blight our land.

It was 1980 not 1445 or 1645 but 1980 I just did not understand this aversion to our way of life yes, we are different we choose not to worship their god preferring our nature-based ways and opening to spirit. Why is it so wrong to be true to yourself? This is why we hide it from them. Fear can destroy worlds.

The far field

It was now 1982 we decide to clear the back field where the old green houses were taking a scythe from the outbuilding, we sharpened it. It sliced through grass and brambles like they were tissue paper we covered a lot of that field in just one morning with 2 scythes

We ran a market stall now veg from our plot, we kept what we needed sold the rest which paid for other things we needed repaired we intended to repair these greenhouses and use them once we had cleared the land.

My girls were playing with the dogs in the cut down part of the field rolling in the cut down grass we had burnt the thistles and other stuff in a fire. We had no idea we were not connected to the main sewer system. I had stepped onto what was a cess pit fell in up to my thighs in shit and piss, all my husband could do was laugh he was in hysterics he even had tears running down his face as I screamed get me out of here this pit must have been six foot deep and square shaped the covering must have rotted. Imagine the stench of 2 years old sewage clinging to your body yuk but he pulls me out eventually them said take everything off outside the barn we need burn it then get a shower and redress I will burn them and then phone the council about getting them emptied. Two whole years we have lived there, and they did not tell us that is if they even knew themselves. They did not so we found three more of these on our land all connected to the east garden sewer pipes. The next day they came to empty them put some stuff in them to destroy the smell. Then told us they one come monthly.

My husband spent the day busting into fits of laughter as we continued clear the field we got to over the other side near the boundary between our land and Sid's land. When we hit something hard. We moved the brambles to find an old packing trunk when I say old it had to be from the 1600s it was blue with steel clasps and a lock on it, we smashed this off with a hammer. We opened it slowly the lid was lined in blue fabric but the stench coming from it made us step back, this top layer contained a Childs rag doll with a faded blue dress just like Tanith's raggedy Annie. Then a book of papers that as the air hit them dissolved into pieces, the doll had wool hair in ringlets it had a faded blue dress and these bloomers to its ankles and boots its eyes were buttons of wood. It was pretty 2 knives were in here of African make they looked like voodoo knives. We took them out placed them in a box then as we went to lift the lower lid the smell became rancid and we stood away dropping it back down looking at each other we open doors go the house to chat about it get a stiff drink. We had no idea what could be inside this box, we suspected a dead pet or just old stuff that had been abandoned a long time ago. We stood in the kitchen talking about this find we took a brandy and sank it down then decided to go look before dark. We took a long blade and went back to the chest we placed masks over our mouth and nose, then slowly pulled the lid up again, that smell came out as the air hit it, we poked about in the chest and a feather quilt was wrapped about something we found a bone mike said it's a dog laughing at me, then we pulled another bone and dropped it fast that was not a dog's bone, that was a human bone or looked human. We slammed the lid shut locked it so our children would not try open it. Going back inside we decided the next day to go talk to Sid whose family had lived on this land since 1600s.

That night the house was the worst it had been ever before all the windows and doors opened and shut and banged there was this banging on the walls and a foul wind came through the house over and over again like some creature was running wild through our place it was so bad the fire went out, our lights all burst and tripped the power

The dolls pram was at the top of the stairs and it came down them I grabbed Morgan as she was sitting on the steps talking to her dolly. But it caught her head in the corner it was not deep, so I dressed it. We lit candles but they blew out the only safe place in the house was the temple room, so I went upstairs to grab blankets I decided we were safer in there as I was not really sure what was happening. I climbed up our stairs clinging to the handrail as this wind blew me and the banging on the walls got louder and louder till you needed put your hands over your ears. Getting to the girl's room it was peaceful there incredibly quiet indeed excepting the Lego and dolls house were in a pile with the beds upturned on their heads, just floating in the air like they were held by invisible string.

I made it back down and we all went inside the temple where we cast a circle and asked the gods for help. My lady came to me she looked so beautiful her hair so long and lovely she had her bow slung over her shoulder arrows in a quiver and her shoes oh my god I wanted those shoes they were gold and like these sandals that tied up her legs. She had a man with her I had not seen before he was a warrior his weapons told their own story. They stood there looking at me she said to remain there till dawn that it would all be quiet then but that the damage may be caused by the opening of the chest, that we must find out what is in it and discover when it was put there as it could well be a witchcraft rite done a very long time ago in which case, we would not be able to do anything about it without knowing what was done or how she said the papers that dissolved may well have been the ritual itself.

We slept soundly that night in here with our fire lit and candles incense burning it was so safe and nice to just be together and lay down as a family the goddess said our family light was bright and nothing could harm us not really but the house had its own issues. That maybe I needed help it. I asked how she said smiling I will not tell you the answer find it.

We woke refreshed and well the house was noticeably quiet indeed but a huge mess our lounge furniture was upended, and books were strewn around the floor our curtains lay on the floor with snapped poles. The kitchen was a bigger mess every plate we had was broken, the pans were all on the floor. The table covered in dirt like earth upstairs was just the same furniture all ruined or broken. It was like someone had a massive temper fit.

We did some digging into the history of the house whilst the children were with their nana,

In 1176 the land was arable land described as Merton 12 12 it was called Merton 12 94 it was called marten rich arable land with 13 tide cottages 1 manor house in 1416 it was the same except it said the manor was the magistrate's house. By 1645 it said Merton was arable land with 13 tide cottages and 1 manor house of the squires / magistrate he had 2 wives and 2 children the bishop of bicoham would stay there breaking his journey to Lytham manor.

Sleeping was hard as it was plagued by dreams of this house in the far past a woman in white ran down the corridor being chased by a man wearing riding gear, he was hitting his side with a crop she runs to that really old door to find it locked she turns runs down the other corridor he was after her she was screaming leave me alone you vile brute. He laughs I never saw his face only hers she was a young woman maybe 20 or something like that maybe even younger.

It jumps to the bedroom my bedroom but in the past the bed in the same place as mine candles lit the room on that same dresser we reused from the attic. Women in black dresses were there the woman is screaming in labour, there was far too much blood the woman in charge said she was bleeding far too much she had ripped open as the child came its legs all twisted up but it cried they wrapped it up throwing rags on the fire but minutes later the mother died, they covered her head left the bed covered in blood and dirty linen taking the child away they talked to the man he threw a fit at them saying take that squawking thing away from me I will not accept that thing as mine my son was born healthy so why not this girl she cannot be mine. Remove it get it a wet nurse put it in the attic room. Away from me I do not want to see it or hear it yes Master they said bowing to him. They must have been servants because the midwife had gone. I woke up

Was I seeing the past a child is born who loses its mother, the girl on the stairs with the callipers on her legs cried for her mother every night?

I went to see Sid on his land he was in his kitchen drinking tea, come in lass sit down tea dear yes please what can I do for you? Well, we have been clearing the land near the old green houses to access the land there, but we found an old chest against the boundary wall.

Sid went pale stammering thou did not open it lass did thee, tell me thee did not please lass. You have seen it has not the lass it near but destroyed the place the last time. you mean the thing that ravaged my house last night something big and angry we slept in our temple room the place is a mess down there. But did the open its lass? Yes, we did what did thee find? Not much some papers that dissolved in the light of day a doll and well some bones we shut it and locked it decided come see you. I dreamt of my place last night and a woman in a white gown being chased by a man with a riding crop, she birthed a baby that wasn't right she died and he wouldn't see it had it put up in attic room didn't want be disturbed by it.

Well lass I can show thee better than tell thee come into the oldest part of my house lass the part that is tiny. My family bought the cottage and all my land from the Templars. They were leaving so sold it all on my family had money but not enough buy the manor as a whole. You are aware this land has always been pagan land never Christian land. Yes, I said well come the 1600s when the burning times came, we hid from them but the Lord he was the magistrate and oft had to engrain some of our own but we made sure they had potion so they could not tell them anything. We told them to say yes, they worshiped the devil signed his book danced about with him in the dark, took herbs to fly. It was a fantasy story as you know but why tell them anything more as once taken you were as good as dead as you also know. IN the 1600s your place dominated the land acres of lush farming land, for miles about nothing else but these 13 cottages and that house. Can you imagine our track lass and the main road all muddy and cut with cart tracks and carriages of the rich no markets excepting Lytham and Bisphosam each of them more than 20 miles away from here? So, people had to trek for two days on foot with a hand cart to sell their stuff at market once a month. He showed me maps of the land his family had and it was bigger than now, they had sold some back to the Lord of the manor. He showed me pictures of his family hand drawn sketches he had of his great grandfather. He said he would tell me the story he was told as a lad of 16 years old taking over the land.

Sid's Story. I canna say if this be a true account lass as these knows time distorts most things till, we know nothing of them times no more as most folks here about never learned to read or write, so stuff was by word of mouth told in stories and passed down that way. The lady died young of a fever and the boy was distraught he was so young then he needed a mother's love so the Master married again to a woman from another rich family she spoilt the child fed all his fantasy he was sent away to school as young as 8 years we didn't see him again till he was grown at 15 by then he had changed beyond belief he hated us poor folk with a vengeance he would ride all the time beat the horses and servants be very demanding of them. He had London manners now he was no longer one of us he had been baptised into the church faith in London his father hated him now sent him away to work so we did not see him again for a long time till the master died. Then he came home with a young woman said she was his wife he was but 20 then, he was a nasty piece of work his lady did not ride horses herself she was far too refined for that. He hated it she was given a horse taught to ride it he was demanding and cruel she fell one day when riding in the fields she refused to ride again. The Master was furious with her drinking and getting very drunk he would chase her through the house wanting his conical rites, but he wanted to beat her first with his riding crop she was heard by the servants and next day tended by them. One night in his stupor she was running to the older parts of the manor he after her we would hear her screams most nights up here. She bore him a son after this he calmed down, he loved that boy so much he taught him his father's way with the land and became a pagan again he became kind and good to the people of the land then one year the crops failed and we all but starved to death he had to keep face with the rich as if he was ok so he had parties and dances and food flowed that we really needed for the winter. But he had to keep face. Many of the poor in the village died that year, he fed who he could his workers but no more. He had studied our ways and yet he had this battle inside of him about them he was often heard to say it was so different from the ways of the church. But he Mastered it led us all at the rites and passionately believed he had to provide for us. His wife was having another child but this one was not right the midwives says it was twisted small thing. we never ever saw it but once with her in the garden it could not walk just crawl drag itself about on the grass. A few years later our harvest failed again worse than last time. This time cattle died from lack of hay horses had to be slaughtered for meat. We had no bread no nothing many of the village died come spring the master said we had to do a rite the old way we were not sure as we had not sacrifice for a long time to the gods, he devised a rite to feed the land he said he would provide what was needed, the people came and at the rite an animal was brought forth, a huge hunting dog from his dogs then he carried the girl child she was drugged and asleep.

They killed the dog cut it in half placed half in the chest half was buried in the large back field He killed the girl and once dead she was cut in half and the same was done it was so top and bottom were made up from child and animal. He said the parts buried would feed the land from the inside the part on top would feed the land from above. We had the best harvest we had ever had we were sworn to secrecy that none who knew the rite would talk My great grandfather was one of them. He was very old at the time died shortly after as did most of them of some strange fever we never knew if they were poisoned, we were told that it was placed near the boundary and was to be left in peace they created a guardian spirit for the land lass. But these days we know nothing of what they did but these base stories we do not know if it were true or not, we have no writings at all from then everything was burnt in the 1600s because of the fear nothing from then but scraps have survived. We have an old book my family kept but there is no mention of guardian rites. If I could help the lass best, I can offer is we do a protection rite for the lass at the next moon. I said thank you a few months later Sid died of a stroke his son took over the land. We opted to leave things be as we did not know what was true so had to leave it alone

After we had left for two years, we heard nothing then we could hear the spirit calling to us So we went to the house the land had all been ripped up by diggers and the stables were all gone along with all the out buildings the house well the conservatory was gone half the kitchen gone we stepped inside Tanith was about to run into the lounge when I saw what was now there the beast had turned into a hateful creature which was extremely strong its land ripped to pieces for a road. I held her back saying we cannot help Tanith was upset she was talking to it. But it was no longer a child. I asked what it wanted us to do it said take the bones and bury them where they will not be disturbed. We knew Sid's land had a protection order on it, so we took the bones buried them at the edge of his land. The spirit seemed happier when we left it nodded at us saying thank you. It was all we could do for it Seeing the; land we loved so ripped up really hurt us both as we loved that spirit of the land so much. We think it called on us knowing we would come to see it. Knowing how we respected the craft. Knowing we would help it.

Screaming trees

Whispers of the Witch by NanyWytch

Bartle's wood is an ancient place full of tress and rocks, genuinely nice place for a walk and for sitting. I loved it there one day I could hear all this screeching from over here it was just after dawn exceedingly early. I walked over trees were being ripped from the earth by diggers and piled in a huge pile baby sapling to incredibly old trees indeed. The screeching was them they were being murdered by the hundred. Some of the trees were being turned to sawdust to be bagged up to sell others were just left in this pile near the gate. The trees most sensitive part is in the roots not the branches we are taught to respect them. To talk to the tree spirits that reside in them. Most trees are friendly only an odd one or two are not and usually it is to do with how they are treated by humans we are the most destructive creatures I know of our beautiful planet. I walked amongst the trees in the pile saw a silver birch sapling with no roots at all I picked it up I could feel it was still alive but just I found the roots thrown into another pile I took them told the trees I was going to take this to serve the goddess that if the tree spirits wanted to live, they have to come into the tree I was taking that I couldn't save them all, but these few would be made into beautiful staffs for magical work. I felt a surge of energy come to me I was happy that we could save these. I spoke to the men they told me they had orders to clear a pathway as a girl had been murdered there and a huge police operation was ongoing to find the killer. Taking them back to RBB we talked about the trees, we began making them into staffs and wands but the roots that had been separated we turned into a dryad for me they are earth spirits if you were not aware. Forests are a great place to learn about elementals they want to serve mankind with the hope of one day gaining a soul to live in them. You can learn to talk to them but respect them for whom they are. We made three staffs that day. Mine has a snake head as I like snakes and is the silver birch one RBB said it was immensely powerful. He asked me what was in it I said. You will wake him up too early he is t healed yet. Ok so you are not going to tell me then I said NO We talked about this murder, watching the news it was nasty unbelievably bad indeed and so close to the house. The very next morning we hadn't been up long when the police arrived at the house wanted search the place, they saw RBB and saw his beard a witness had said the killer has grey hair and a grey beard, guess they thought they had found him so early into the investigation they questioned RBB and the rest of us Sarah his daughter Rhoda his wife and Me his student. At the time RBB was a lecturer at Leeds university he was well respected and well known in magical circles told them he may be able to help them by contacting spirits to see if they knew anything it was 1981 the police laughed went away the next weekend, they were back they said yes to help they were stuck. RBB had not been told anything about the crime scene at all he did his thing told them the girl was 10 and described her very well, he said the killer knew her well she talked to him sat with him. Later he killed her with a long blade maybe an army type knife for survival. It was in a green case on his belt, he described the crime scene, down to the last detail then shocked them by saying the killer is hiding in those woods still he is camped there near the rocks. So, they left knowing his name and where they may find him the killer was found the next day. The case was over after 3 weeks, in return the council created what is now named as Bartle wood Bartle is part of RBB name as his name was Richard Bartle Bitelli. he had spoken about magic in Italy being against the law as its run by the Vatican and Mafia. Thinking on tree spirits you ought never take a branch from a tree or indeed blossoms have you not asked for them, teaching others is fraught with dangers. I had a young student whom to me was a very girly girl. However, he was a gay lad problem being to me he was also someone I knew from before but could not recall where. Anyway, I told him its best make your own wand from a tree so that the tree spirit blesses it with embed life force. I explained not to steal it but to give the gift if silver something of your own for its exchange of one piece of branch remember it is a living thing. Well, a few days go by and he calls me up in such fear for his life. Saying he is being attacked at night by this tree. I smile to myself realising he has not listened to a word I said about tree spirits. I had to bring him to me, take him back to the woods and yet still we did not appease the tree spirit but inside the temple that night we saw why. At the ritual feasting Alan began to gorge himself with biscuits he could not stop eating them. We said you will be sick no he said nice. I noticed he was not alone the tree spirit had followed him back to ours it decided as he had taken its peace it would take from him. I was amused at seeing a person possessed by the spirit of a tree. I explained to it that it had to go back to the woods as it did not belong here. Stay it said can do more. No I said you cannot stay inside Allan he is sorry for the harm he caused you and will heal your limb make recompense by taking care of you silver it said he did not give me gifts. He did not speak with me at all. He is no witch, yes I said he is a baby like your sapling is. So, I go home now he comes cares for my baby he takes her home till she is safe. I agreed as for Allan he was terrified to even venture near the oak tree afterwards, so we took it upon ourselves to take care of that sapling.

I read people seem to think they can pick up fallen twigs from the ground for wands however these will be brevet of spirit by asking for a live piece spirit will be shared with you.

It will live on inside your wand be great service to you but once you no longer need it. It is best to take it to the earth and bury it to allow that spirit to return to the earth.

My staff is very powerful it has a beak with eyes and a mouth hair is horse hair beads and feathers to decorate he looks great one-year I was visiting another coven when at their rite the priestess said she was going do a spell against a witch whom had moved into the area. I said that I cannot loan my powers to this so may I leave the circle please I know this woman has just lost her husband. She is an author; witch &mother I think you are wrong to work against her when she has not harmed any of you. Minutes later her priest joined me. We were talking about a vision I had about one of their covens when suddenly a spirit spoke through him saying he needs your help you must go today.

Then he was back asking me what had just occurred having told him, he was genuinely concerned the convener was not at the rites due to moving to a new house.

Later having decided visit on the morrow, as everyone had drunk quiet a lot of wine, so driving was out really. I went to bed, was just falling asleep when my angels woke me said come here listen and watch. So, I did what I saw annoyed me some, she was doing a poppet blessing it as me to make me sick and ill, because I had asked leave the rite. I watched her do the spell saw where she hid the poppet once the house was quiet, I went down took the poppet removed the cord and pins re blessed it then placed it back. The next morning, I come bounding down the stairs loads of energy very well. She looks at me quiet oddly says do you feel OK, yeah why? Oh no reason I thought you looked peaky yesterday are you sure. Of course, I replied but I am going to leave today as I am missing the girls. Might I use the altar before we leave, of course you may. I placed my staff at the side of the altar, said whenever she does dark magic against another without good reasons you are to stop it. I will bring you back in 3 moons. Then we left during the next month I was told all the electrics in the house blew. The following month the house flooded; she became frightened of my staff as she thought it were alive. It is of course, but notes she thought so she took it outside tied to a tree running up the outside wall. Then on the 3rd moon a big storm hit with thunder she said my staff ate the lightening, but it was not damaged at all, but the wall gave way at side of her house. She was convinced my staff was doing all this stuff. So, she took my staff to my teacher's house who put him outside attached to his oak tree. He was watching the storm that night when lightning struck his tree burning it down one side the second fork went straight into my staff. He phoned me saying Ash love what is in your staff? Trees, what? anyway it is here as your coming down, but it eats lightening yeah I said it will be ok yes, he says but my tree is not, it will be ok if my staff is there trust me. Once at his place a couple of days later Richard had brought my staff in shocked as his tree had recovered from the storm. It was fine. So, he was puzzled too so when I arrive, he says what did you put inside the staff.? Nothing I say the trees did it themselves. What? Listen to it? He held him putting it near him he said whispers. Yes, and he is a great dancer so I showed Richard how he can dance with me holding the tip of my finger at his beak so he could gyrate.

RBB said it healed my tree and it seems you have half a wood in there. Yes, I said I think so but at least the spirits are safe now. Exactly he nodded.

Stone the Wytch

Authors note This chapter is about persecution witches have always been targets of the church for a long time because in 1474 pope innocent v111 decreed our religion to be heresy. Churches were then built over the top of our pagan sites; we were banned from worshipping our gods forced to attend mass in a church built by pagans. In 1612 pope Gregory consolidated the church anyone charged with witchcraft would lose all their property and monies to the church. This is how they became wealthy. Burning and hanging anyone accused of heresy. This act was repelled in 1739 with the fraudulent mediums act still used today.

Whispering walls was as you know on the pagan side of the road and the priests feared it, so they stayed away. Which was great for us we were left alone to practice our crafte.in 1983 maybe around Ostara we were given a visitor a woman claiming she would be a witch practice our craft. When questioned more she said she would be a good servant to the devil and obey him. We sent her back to the church. now many days later I was collecting my children from the school like lots of mums do every day. The place was crowded as always, I came out of the gate holding my girl's hands near the corner was that girl with a few of her friends. She started to shout devil worshippers devil worshippers stone them they need to die the group with her started to throw stones at me and the girls I turned about to head back into the school but the priest closed the gate on me standing there looking on laughing at me. The crowd grew bigger they were all throwing stones at me I got hit in the head my girls were hit too I wrapped my coat around them I knew I couldn't go home as they may follow me but I had nowhere to go till an old man said come he took me and the girls into his house around the corner shouting at these people stop this hateful behaviour you ought to be ashamed called yourself catholic. The crowd came around to this man's house his wife was lovely around 80 years old she gave us a drink and fed my children some cakes. Then the mob started to break down the gate then they smashed the windows of the house the old lady said come we went to the yard she shouted to Eiffel take these children over the wall to yours can you see that mob they are trying kill them. They called the police I was in there house my girls next door I called my husband to come from work told him come around the back.

We phoned the police who said they would come but right now if nobody were hurt there was nothing they could do.

They finally broke down the door with an axe obviously they had gone to gather weapons to complete the job by time they got into the house mike as there. They attacked him pushing him into the narrow stairwell so he could not fight back the old guy was on the phone again to the police saying they are attacking the woman's husband now they are going to kill us all.

They came into the lounge and hit the old man on the head with a wooden stick he fell down hurt his head bleeding the old lady they hit over the head too then went after me I fought back kicking and punching I grabbed the axe and hit one of them in the face I pushed them out the door before I was knocked out by one of them they tried to drag me outside but Mike hit them and pushed them off me we could hear the sirens the old man had got up he took pictures of them with his camera. That girl was the leader of this gang. 30 minutes was like a lifetime to me on that day I feared for my life and my children's. The mob vanished into the dark.

When the police arrived four ambulances were there to take us all to hospital my children were passed back over the wall to us the police said if the photos were good, they could arrest them they asked where the girl lived, I said across the road they all went in there.

They went over to talk to her she was not alone the men were in there as well, so the police arrested them all for criminal damage with assault and battery. They said we needed to stay away from the house for at least a week as these would get bail tomorrow. Asked if we had somewhere to go, we said we can go stay at my mums for a week. Which is what we did I had broken collarbone and stitches to my head the old man had stitches and broken arm the old lady had broken hip and stitches to her head mike needed stitches to his head Tanith was just bruised and so was Morgan, you could see where the stones had hit them.

We were safe at my mums we kept the girls from school after I told mum the priest slammed the gate shut and laughed as we were being stoned by these good Catholics. She said they cannot go back there now. You need another place if they came down there love they could have killed you all. After 4 days the police came said we needed identify these people they had arrested from the photos they needed to know who did what. So, we went to the station we did the line-ups picked out the men and her from them told the police what they had done with what weapon whom they did it too. We decided as the girls were with my mum we would go to the house. Oh my god my lovely house and land, they had set fire to me veg patches they had burnt down the sheds smashed up the house my furniture was burnt in piles on the floor., my temple room oh dear goddess they had destroyed everything smashed it up set fires on the floor it had slogans all over the walls on black paint. Thou shalt not suffer a witch to live which is a mis translation from, thou must not allow a sorcerer to live this one sentence has killed more witches than we could count. At this point I was so angry but at the same time crying not from fear but from the fact we had managed to not be there so we were safe my dogs were dead hacked to pieces where they were I think the people may have bite marks on them It was destroyed even upstairs was smashed to pieces the girls toys destroyed I cried as I picked up pieces of my life off the floor, my children cried saying mummy why did they hate us we are not bad are we I said no my darlings it's because we are witches they hate us. We decided it was not safe as we knew they had been charged and were then given bail till trial. They were rearrested for damage to council property and killing of two animals the police said we had got away lucky with our lives if we had gone back home, they could have found us hacked to death like our dogs.

We packed what we could into the van and we left to collect the girls we took our dogs to bury them near the chest we asked the guardian to please take them for the sacrifice they had given, at my mums we told her we had arranged go to Macclesfield to mikes mums, we would stay with her till we had a new place live. Witches are good at starting over somewhere else.

Authors note (add other notes re dates of persecution of witches

As no churches were built in England before 597AD, the catholic Church not consolidated till between 544-604AD. Churches were built on top of pagan places of worship in order to get the people to gather there. It was not until 1484 when pope innocent v111 wrote a bull being a sacred order against pagans. By calling their beliefs Heresy word that simply means not of God.   Exodus xx11:18 is a wrong quotation from Greek into Latin then into English. In the old testament there is no mention of witches or indeed a devil. Certainly not the churches idea of the devil or indeed witches kissing one. This is due to the fact that the original bible was Jewish written in Hebrew, they also have no witches in that version. Therefore, the bible has nothing to do with witchcraft, we do not have devils. In the verse in the Hebrew bible

Kaskaghiscau means poisoner obviously as this did not translate well into Latin, they simply omitted it for witchcraft because they wanted rid of the competition. It is well known that only the winners of battles write the history.

Haunting of my sister

Dated 1st February 1982 era vulgurus

These notes are taken from coven books for 1982

1st February 1982

I am overly concerned about the psychological welfare of my sister its increasingly obvious she is not herself she is always so drained of energy she cannot recall things even for a few minutes she is not eating, sleeping and I worry for her psychological physical welfare

3rd February

Worrying increases for my sister's welfare we had consulted a Dr who declared he could find nothing wrong with her medically, psychologically he was concerned prescribed tablets said he found her to be depressed and anxious my sister was always the nervous type

As a baby she was different she rocked backwards forwards on her rocker making this horrible err sound.

That night a storm was raging it was a really bad one the rain was running down the lane like a river,

4th February

Our concerns are now worse the atmospheric balances in our home were even more disturbing than normal something was coming and fast, but we could not see the atmospheric balances in our home were being eradicated this atmosphere is only here when she is around. She went out tonight with a man we did not like he had a weird idea of right and wrong, but it is her life not ours her free will must be preserved.

5th February

Atmosphere in house deteriorating faster now we cleanse and within hours its back. By now the atmosphere in the whole house was darker her moods and temper fit worse. Suddenly she was raging throwing things smashing up her room. I told her to be quiet let the girls sleep her night-time wanderings were out of control. I wanted my parents tell me why they did not want her home. Father said it was none of my business it was now. She went out again with this man we did not like he kept saying he knew what we were into strange as he knew nothing about us at all. I can only describe the feeling as a black panther standing in the darkness just out of view ready to pounce on us without warnings, heavy black clouds are overhead today it was as if we were covered by a thick blanket blocking out the light

Coven members were in the house tonight as we had work to do, I had called them saying that we had to deal with what was happening I sensed something with my sister around her vamping her energy as if she had something clinging to her back.

We tried to help her by pampering her today painting nails doing hair girly stuff, but her mood was very dark suddenly she started to scream at me you don't love me you don't care about me at all you have your own life and it's not mine I am not part of your stuff. I should not be living here I should be at home. They do not want me there at all nobody wants me She then stormed out of the house without shoes or indeed a coat in just her nightdress. We tried to follow her, but we lost her past the stables somewhere, I said to coven she will come back but we need be ready as she is not alone tonight. There has to be a reckoning, some of the men went out seeking her, Mike said maybe she is gone home. No such luck I said once dad throws you out, you are not going back in his beliefs are you obey his rules, or you do not reside there called RBB talked to him about thus build-up of behaviours the content night-time mood swings. He said it sounds like she is possessed by a spirit, but you will not know what type till you're doing the exorcism, remember sometimes the dead don't know they are dead, sometimes they become violent because they seek attention they had when alive. Being on your land it could be anything, but it will all stem from the cause of the falling out with your father. Now larval entities are indeed baby demons the lowest form, at around midnight she appeared outside standing like a drowned rat staring at us like she was not even present. Concerned about her dying from exposure I dragged her inside removed her wet clothing and wrapped her up in new night gown socks dressing gown sat her near the fire. but she fought me like some kind of hell cat scratching hissing biting screaming. Her language was vile her strength quiet a lot more than she normally had as a petite size 8

Then she grabs my hair us pulling my head backwards with some force a voice came from her that was foul it stank. Then I was thrown halfway up the room I am going to kill you bitch do you hear me your dead you cannot stop me I am going to beat your brains out all over the floor.

, I pushed her onto the sofa then was thrown about 6ft away from her. I will beat your stupid brains out witch get the fuck off me. Now that was not my sister. I got up went straight back sat astride her on the sofa pushed her backwards. Just at that moment Susan started to bang the doors & windows she was disturbed did not like the intrusion into its place. A child's voice said it has to die it is not right it is not right killed it now it has to be now then jeans voice helps me help me it has got to go I don't want this help me before it's too late. She opens her eyes her face distorted it was not even her to begin with I do not know where my sister was at all, but this was not her. Where is my sister it laughs with me do you want her back then she is a dirty little whore she should be killed or put down?

It will not let me as it wants to stay. Next thing I know she had a knife and was trying stab her stomach I pushed a cushion in the way she was stabbing it over and over had she been alone she might have killed herself. Her eyes had gone a yellow colour it said it must die kill it kill it, it started fall asleep I woke it up slapping my sisters face it laughs you cannot hurt me only her you are not resting on my watch demon you will stay here I took the knife from her grasp giving it to pat. I washed her face talked to her saying I know you are tired week, but you must fight this jean, you must face it not run away from it fight it jean come on we cannot help if you don't fight. I had washed my hands in consecrated water it said get that filthy shit off me I asked Phil to call RBB again as I was unsure what else I needed to do bring her back to us He said we are watching you don't worry you're doing ok keep going now do you know blood magic's in your style I said yes why use it know you have enough of you there cut them add the blood together link to a circle around her then grab

her hands hold her do not let go the power needs to stay focused and central you are now using your souls' power.

We swept the floor around her with our brooms clearing away the negate energy then we interlocked our hands the whole coven which at this time was 8 people 4 of them family. putting her in the middle on the floor, we had tried carry her into the temple but that failed it could not cross the threshold. So, the lounge had to do sage was used she was now so weak she was not fighting, it was going to win. give me the knife, I blessed it with consecrated water fire. Then I cut my hand, passed it about we poured wine dropped drops into the wine each cut their own hand adding to the chalice then taking hold of each other we reached for her we said the blood of the family is strong together my sister is ours drink of our blood.

Blood of our blood return back to us now, Jean said it is too hard I cannot we replied blood of our blood we can do anything now push it out we are here you are our blood. Nothing can stop you now use our strength to help you connect to the blood. It is our life force now fight. Suddenly she was back with us 3 days later she came to me crying said I think I started my period, but something came out of me in the night she had wrapped it into tissue. It looked like a malformed foetus of around 5 months. We burnt it on the fire this pure black smoke went straight up the chimney with a weird screech.

Not long after this jean went back home as a not so innocent girl I asked her about it, she told us in coven so what caused the issue has to remain in the coven books.

Authors note:

In possession there are 3 stages I do not think my sister came till the later stage.

Infestation the bangs noises disturbed sleep things being moved about or thrown.

Oppression the lower demons will attach to the victim, them as the higher one comes, they detach. The demon will then mentally torment its victim these mental attacks take many forms. It cannot possess until its victim is weak.

Possession now it can move into the body mimic the person very well however close family will notice something is not right. As demons never hug or kiss, they do not understand the human need of emotional contact.

Larval entities are inferior they try to obtain life in matter denser to their own which brings about the infectious unbalanced behaviours that family would pick up on as abnormal to that person's soul nature. Now once the original is pushed aside it is the larval that controls the body pushing the original host to the side or expelling them from the body

We cannot help them till they reach what we call crisis point just as the real essence is taking over the person. Remember demons do not need a body to live they are omnipotent beings they do not belong in our realm.

Mirror on the wall.

We had moved to Macclesfield the home of my husband's family. We had been given a 3 bedroom ground floor flat near the park on a estate called Vicky park, it was a upstairs flat but was big inside as you go into the door a space existed below the stairs for coats and prams, then at the top of the stairs was the first bedroom it was long and narrow well not that narrow about 10ft wide but a lot smaller than we had at the manor, around a corner was a long hallway from which all other room were off the bathroom was at the top of the corridor on your right the girls room was also right it was big then our room was the back bedroom which was ok not very big but large enough. The lounge was long and quite wide the kitchen was ridiculously small indeed no room for a table. So, I placed a safety gate at the edge of the long corridor leading to the stairs this separated the temple room from all other rooms. We had rescued a few things but for the most part everything had to be replaced but I still had my book of shadows and athame as I had taken them with me along with my robes and staff, we had clothing as they had not burnt these.

Once we had settled in rebuilt a temple, we were ok we had got the girls into school at the top of the hill puss bank school. It was a great school, so they were happy Tanith mostly as she had her cousin who was one month older these two became inseparable in the coming months and years. I had created a guardian for the temple he was an eternal warrior with a red plume on his helmet he rode a black horse and had a sword and axe plus knives he was told what his job was and linked to me. This warrior was possibly the reason most temple things were just in a pile on the floor not burnt. Although our furnishing had not survived the smaller things did.

My girls were taught not to go in there without mummy or daddy, mostly they obeyed this rule they were good girls. I had found it hard to conceive for over 3 years, so I had worked a spell asking the gods to help me they did help me I was now pregnant it was now 1983. We had; left the girls with a teenage babysitter we had got to know her parents and were out with them at the time only at the local pub down the road about ten minutes' walk from the house. At 10pm I get a phone call at the bar my girls are saying come home now we need you. Obviously, we went straight back I was mobbed by both girls it was gone 10.30pm now I had expected them to be fast

asleep but no they were on hyper drive and shouting at the same time. I asked them to calm down so I could understand why there was no babysitter Tanith said mummy Tracy said that there was no guardian to get her that it was just a bedroom and that you had lied to us so she went into your room with all her clothes on and her trainers too but after a few minutes the door opened and the trainers came out of there flew down the stairs then a few more minutes and she was dragged out by your warrior thrown down stairs and out the front door. She ran away mummy the warrior smiled at us winked and went back into the temple mum my he is really real we saw him he is big, and he is real. Yes, darlings I said he is now. I phoned her parents to tell them that she had defiled our temple they were terribly upset to know their own daughter had done something of this nature them being witches too.

We use mirrors as doors to the magical realms in my temple I had two dark mirrors one at each end of the room they did not exactly face each other I did not want to create a corridor but access to my warrior and for the gods.

We all wear masks to survive in this realm we use a simple way to really see yourself we sit down before a mirror and we speak

Mirror on the wall

Show me up the one and all

Show the true person sitting here

Make my vision true and clear

Mirror on the wall show me up the one and all

It works very well but do not stare into the mirror, gaze into it your face will start to change be prepared to see the real you. I am quite old have a scar down my face on the left side one of my eyes has a scar going from my eye to my face on right side, yet I am still pretty and very pale skin red hair. I have a big scar on my left shoulder. In this life I do not have those scars they were from a previous life when I was tortured and hung, I now have an aversion to anything tight about my neck. I also have a fear of water in this life after they tried drowning me.

I had got to know a few people now taken my girls to the local play group sometimes, it was a flat around the other side of the estate it had a play group with nursery nurses it had two social workers who were available to help out plus a mum's room where they could go have coffee and chat to other mums make friends create things. We were all knitting squares to make blankets for the elderly as xmas gifts we thought those who lived alone having no family would maybe not get a gift at yuletide so our idea was to ensure the people local to us all got one gift a blanket they could have on their sofa or chair to help keep them warm. These gifts were all made at the start of the year giving us time to make as many as we could. Any spare would be given to hospitals for the elderly there. There was a nice guy couple lived near us, we got to know them very well, the girly one Greg was funny he was one who behaved like a fussy woman cleaning & cooking a lot. But their flat was absolutely gorgeous. The bedroom was small, but they had mirrored tiles on the ceiling, drapes around the bed it was very romantic with a portrait of them both on the wall. The lounge was so neat and tidy it could be a picture in a magazine. Greg came to the playgroup with us a few times, then the social workers banned him from coming in. When we asked why they said he was gay they could not risk him being near the children. We complained about this in protest we stayed away holding play parties at mums houses instead. The social worker got sacked, the play group reopened. Things were so different in the 80s to now, sometimes I think people are rather pampered now

Playing with Demons can harm you

At the playgroup one day in the mum's room a woman approaches me sits down next to me most people on the estate had known I was a witch Read tarot, runes did party bookings made creams and tinctures. She said as the other mums were watching, they told me you may be able help me that you do things to clean houses of things. my flat is being taken over by something its very frightening, I am worried for my children she had two small boys who were here today along with many other children off the estate.

When someone comes to a witch saying something like this, we know very well that, that something was invited in by them. We consider carefully what move to make with everything we do. I was 4 months gone now so I had to think of myself and child first. I said I would come to her flat take a look with her, whilst the children played but would not do anything at this stage just take a look.

Her flat could be seen from the playgroup window she pointed out her window of her bedroom hers was a downstairs flat these flats were organised on one up one down rotation with long corridors and stone stairwells lifts at the end where the bin sheds were, they could be very dark places. Winchester court was where she lived as we were looking at her windows the curtain lifted up as if a hand had taken hold of it so they could see out. I said who is in your flat right now nobody she said it is just me and the boys, but that thing watches me all the time it must know where I am. What I am doing this is what scares me the most it knows things all the time.

We walked towards Winchester court, watched the window as I got closer it was watching it knew I was coming. Talk about the spider and the fly I started to think I may be lunch. Second before we arrived at her door it opened all on its own. it was like saying oh do come in, we are expecting you. she said it does this all the time. We walked down the stairs to the glass door which also opens by itself, into the hall these flats are different to mine this had one long hall that everything comes off, as you turn right it's the lounge and a small area; leading to the bathroom, then back off the corridor on the left is another area leading to the front bedroom, there were two arm chairs tied up here with washing line cord fastened to door handles. Of the two storage cupboards I wondered why a person would do this technically sealing off a larger bedroom. A bit strange but everyone to their own thing, I was just taking it all in whilst watching and feeling my way. I sensed something watching me from in front of me in this hall it was stood near the main bedroom just past the children's room it was in the shadows do but I did not get a clear view.

On the way to the kitchen where she had gone the pictures came down from the wall, they did not break they just dropped, donna said oh yeah that happens a lot. I just put them back is all if they break, I replace them. We went into the large kitchen diner the actual kitchen area was same size as mine, but they had this huge area for dining table we did not have. But I preferred my place as we did not need rely on the lifts or the stairs. In the kitchen we sat down I asked her a few simple questions my first being when did it start? 3 months ago, now she said it happened very slowly but now it is started to invade my sleep. I am so tired I just need to sleep is all. I asked her what you did that started all this if you lie to me, I will not help you so the truth please. Well, I went to a party and some friends had this board they said we could talk to spirits with it, I was a bit sceptical, but it worked, and I found the ring. The next day we did it again but here and it worked again I found the paperwork I was missing. Then when my friend left her board with me saying I needed it more than her I began using it every day once my boys were asleep. I explained to her she had opened a door inside this flat and we needed to close it because she was in what we called virtual entrapment. She asked what it meant I said has your behaviours changed recently yes, she said I am angrier and more aggressive my mother says I am rude and nasty minded. I smiled at her as I could now see the thing standing right behind her hands on her shoulders whispering to her. It was male it was tall and had a beard and dark eyes and it looked straight at me smiled and said to me MINE not yours the whisper came straight into my head it smiled at me saying LEAVE Witch this is mine. I did not feel threatened but then it said err mm fresh life no soul yet yes, I like that. I said well you cannot have it because it is not cooked yet. Aww it said pity, but she is mine I do not want her boys just her she will do nicely. Donna could not hear us she was in a kind of daydream.

I said shall we go back now get the children I can come round later so we can talk more if you like yes, she said please I do not want to be alone. We collected our respective children then parted company I went home talked to my husband about it and we decided that I would go round later on spend a few hours there then come home.

Whispers of the Witch by NanyWytch

I returned about 6pm to Donnas just as it was going dark nice time really, I had taken precautions for myself I had done a ritual for protection so had not gone alone in a spiritual sense. I had things with me we might need, and I was prepared for a fight. As I got there the door opened again, I shouted at the top of the stairs for Donna, she did not hear me or was not there no idea, but I walked down the stairs to the glass door it opened again without me touching it. I was expected again as I walked to the kitchen because I could hear the boys and Donna were there. The pictures flew at me I had to keep ducking to not be hit by glass as it smashed against a wall Donna heard this came to the kitchen door said run so quickly ran to the door and inside the kitchen. The boys were eating Donna made a drink in this quiet space. We talked she said she needed to go out for two hours drop the boys at her mums, I could either come back at 8pm or stay whilst she did it. I thought yeah, I will stay here alone see what is really going down in this place. She asked me would I be ok there I said yes, no worries. So, she left with her boys she said it might be 7.30pm to 8pm before she was home if you get bored just leave and come back tomorrow. The house was now just us; I went to make a drink in the kitchen area this draw flew open all the cutlery flew out the draw aimed at me I grabbed a tray then said missed. A cupboard door ripped off its hinges and flew straight at me I moved it dropped onto the floor awe I said is this all you can do I can do better myself such kinder garden magic wow I expected better. I walked over the broken glass and mess in the hall to the lounge it was nice in there, but the temperature was dropping quickly. In there I sat near the fire trying to get warm but it still kept getting colder so I go to the lounge door it was stood right there looking at me, I said you are very rude you throw things at your guests and call it a welcome. Jeez that is not how you do it, I can show you. Good evening, I am the local witch, I called in to visit you specially wanted another chat if you do not mind. It grunted at me well an introduction would be nice my name is and then we chat, NO it said you can go now well actually I thought to wait for Donna, no Witch we do not want you here so leave. Sorry I cannot do that, I shut the lounge door. The banging on the walls started it was like someone was throwing a hell of a paddy, banging on all the walls at the same time I did not understand why it did not come into the room, I opened the door said What? Is all that noise for? She made a deal with me, she called me here over and over again she wanted me here all the time, so I came each time I left she bought me back again she asked me to be here. She agreed to give me the room with the board, and I give her the lounge as space so we each had alone time. I I lied because yeah, she can be in there but not with the door shut, I want access all the time. Let me get this right you are saying she invited you in here, yes over and over again so now I am here she does not like the game, but she wanted to play the game she agreed to it. She cannot change her mind now. She made the arrangement it was her idea not mine. She cannot say she is innocent. If I go again she will call me back. In order to call you back she must know your name and sigils so have you given them to her. Witches are you crazy why would I give her power over me. Ok just asking, so how long have you been brought here for 4 moons now. What was this agreement between you? She calls on me via the board, says she was very lonely, that she would give anything have some real company. That she liked to talk with me. That if I came into her home she would grant me access to her, and give me my own space, but she needed one room I did not go inside. When I asked which room, she picked the lounge. I did not but I have access via the mirrors she is not a witch look where they are.

I looked yes a doorway; a kind of zig zag corridor could work 8f more than one doorway was opened.

Thanks, I said for that I think I will go home now ok it said leave it opened both doors for me then banged them shut. The next day I went to see her to talk to her about her own actions and the consequences of playing such games with demons. I knew it was there listening to us chatting I could see it standing leaning on a chair right near donna. I said I will put my things in the bedroom then as I am staying over yes, she said I sleep near the door in the bed you can sleep near the window side. I walked into there and the bed mattress was thrown at me I was stuck against the wall with it against my body with something extraordinarily strong on the other side. I wriggled out from under it, went back to the kitchen said right I am fed up with this game now I have decided change the rules, what she said you asked for my help, so I am changing the games rules. But what do you mean? What I said changing the rules you did something you should not have done you made a deal with a demon and expect it to play fair it will not, so I am not either. Come on give me that knife. Why? we are going into the room near the stairs. No, she said you cannot I promised I swore on my life I would not go in there ever. Well, I did not so I started to cut the ropes and move the chairs when she attacked me kicking and screaming like a wild dog. I punched her she fell back onto the floor I turned on her and said do not get up lady or I will put you down again and I do not play nice with others. I am going into the room you are going to c0me with me I cannot then lady I cannot help you. but I need help its raping me in bed at night now please you have to. I said no I do not I did not agree to do anything. I said I would look is all, so I am looking what is going down here. It told me of your insistence it came to you So lady you are coming into the room with me because you are the one keeping it here. I pulled the chairs away and walked into the large bedroom it had a noose hanging from the ceiling a broken chair and a Ouija board with candles around it some paper and pen.

She followed me in crying saying she was sorry; she did not know what she was doing I said ignorance is not a valid excuse darling. Right light the candles for me   I went to seal the door, so nothing went back that way. I called the arch angels in and cast a circle with the board in the middle. I knew the demon was here I could see him I said to him do you want to leave whilst the door is open, I intend to close this door then you will leave via Michael and he does not play nice. It left quickly so I guess it decided not to play with me. So, I broke the board up then burnt it in the bath cleaned up the ashes took them to bury them she screamed the house down. I said listen to me if you bring it back, I am not helping you.

I leave to go home later that night as I am sleeping the guardian came to me saying the spirit of a man who hung himself is wanting you to talk to him. I said no not now send it away. Early next day I woke suddenly Donna I said something is wrong we have to go to Donna's. Taking Phil with me we go to her flat, the front door opens we enter the place is destroyed such a mess broken plates, cups, glasses strewn around the kitchen like a carpet of broken pieces. We walk into the bedroom everything is smashed on the bed lies Donna barely conscious. I talk to her whilst Phil calls an ambulance I say tell me what happened she said it came back it was angry because I could not bear to be alone. It did all this I lost the baby I move the covers blood is seeping out of her legs I say what baby she says the demon's baby we were having sex all the time. I said I think your dreaming this up they are not human they do not have human form never have.

Then a man stood at the door he said I tried to tell you I did try to tell you that she invoked it. It came back angry as hell annoyed at being called again. He destroyed everything even her. Her mind has gone there was no baby at all. She needs help I tried to tell you. But that man with the sword said you would not see me. I need you to help me leave. Where is the demon? In her its inside her now it too late there is nothing to be done.

The ambulance arrives they take her to hospital whispering to herself about demon babies. She had been out bought another Ouija board the demon knew I would not come.

Donna ended up in Parkside mental hospital, her x husband had the boys the family got rid of everything giving up the flat. Donna had played a dangerous game and lost her mind in the process.

I read online many times people telling newbies, its OK to use them. Its not OK unless you know how to use it safely and understand the consequences of opening doors to the spiritual realms. Magick always has a price.

Dolls House Bedford 15th May 1987. 7.30pm

Whispers of the Witch by NanyWytch

Ashna senses a spirit male around 30 years old in pain from twisted limbs needs help. A small of short stature is perceived his hands arms and face contorted out of line to his contour. He is begging for help then Ashna sees another man Danny the new owner of the doll's house his moving in day was 3 days ago. Danny is ill at ease not knowing what to do he calls out Astrally to the coven to come to him now its urgent.

Background

My vision that night was noticeably clear we had to go to the doll's house as a covener was in trouble. Three days previous I had been sitting at the window gazing onto the street of my friend's house when I saw a cobbled road appear then Roman Soldiers marching down it a whole legion of them the noise was loud from all these men marching to where I had no idea. Ashna was ill at ease kept looking outside as if she were expecting something, she could not explain what or why said I can feel it sense it but not sure what it is.

We visited the man in the new place he had bought where he said the neighbours were very friendly but kept bringing things to him saying this belongs in your cottage please take it back now. He did not understand why they were handing him craft tools. The cottage was one of those picture postcard type of a thatch cottage with 2 gardens of flowers and the picket fence. Reginald sat himself in the winged back chair near the large fireplace, and I sat on the low seat near the window. It felt right I had to be near the window as my vision said something was going to happen tonight.

Reginald volunteered sit in the winged chair near the hearth he suddenly started to do direct voice mediumship, he had not done this before, he said that T-thalamus and the children must be made safe, the soldiers were coming to engain them as witches. We heard the boots of many men arriving at the cottage but saw none. Then the banging on the door so loud so real yet we could not see them

open in the name of the King. Thalamus you need to open the door before we break it down

Reg voice changed his stature his facial feature changed this was a spirit over shadowing him

Spirit one

The magistrate sat there he had no need to run but he was very annoyed that his scribe had brought the witch finders men here to his home so late at night when they ought to have come on the morrow.

Second spirit spoke through Daniel his aura strong one of the wise spirit strong

There is a banging at the door

Only after hearing the feet march down the road to the door then it happens again bang

Open in the name of the King

First spirit opens door

You what dost thou want in my dwelling thus night, where is thy authority to override me the magistrate. Dost, thou know that you have disturbed our evening meal that I has important guests this night. Wouldst thou go on the word of one disgruntled employee who was let go this night his services I no longer needs nor desire.

how dare you disturb me this night am I not the justice here? What dost thou seek here?

Who is here this night demanding the witch finder?

there are only my guests my wife Sarah here with our baby

the scribe declares that you harbour witches here.

A man was dragged into the cottage by the soldiers his hands were jittery, it seemed afraid of Thalamus.

He says you have cursed him twisted his hands so he can no longer scribe.

He says there are witches here we need to ascertain if thee all be witches then we are to engain all of these even they children.

Four soldiers went out towards the back they were searching for something.

My dear man how can I be harbouring witches when I am the justice and sits on the bench for those charged so.

Now get thee gone from this house at this late hour

The cottage door banged shut. We heard boots walking away

. Thalamus sat on the winged chair near his hearth

looking straight at me he said your art a comely wench, might I enquire as to your family yes, Sir but I come from another time to help thee the old ones sent me to aid your troubles Might I ask of you questions please.

Of course, says the first spirit

By what name art thee known Thalamus Hilby Hatton the Justice here welcome lady to my home I trust you like the food offered

Yes, thank you genuinely nice is Sarah your wife?

Yes, she is and a good woman all her days

Who was that scribe? Oh, him William Harding he knoweth I had guests to dinner this night he scribed it in my book himself a week past, yet he dares to bring that witch finder here to my home.

I know that your art of the old ways as the gods sent me hence to you was William too

No n my dear wench he is one of these Christian peoples who claim their god lives high in the sky, but one can never see or indeed speak to.

He listens to the tales of Old women at market day then he spreads his evil lies about to that witch finder who pays him to help find witches here.

Why this day?

I had to sit on the bench my son thalamus terribly upset, he had been taken from his work and questioned tortured by them because of Williams stories I had no way out of it they had said he confessed to being a witch

The atmosphere inside the house drew tight,

Was he condemned by your own hand?

Yes, I had no way out of it the lore of the church dictates heresy is the charge for wise craft they banned our ways over the last 200 years or so they want to be rid of us all so they can take our lands and gold this farm has been in my family 500 years its rich arable land many acres. Over that way lays the Bishop of Rome's palaces he wants my farm as it borders his land lands, they stole from our friends by charging them of this new crime. We are but one small village they have very nearly emptied it of women young and old,

Did they get any other of your family thus day?

Nay I only had the one son and the baby Mary plus my Sarah if you had seen what they had done to my boy

I am aware of what they do in the names of their god.

Why lass thou art so comely thou resemble the goddess, yes have been told this I hope it does not disturb you no lass tis a welcome to me this hard night.

Second spirit why art thee asking all these questions wench and whence hail you by what name art thee known

I am known as Ashna it means light; the old ones sent me here to offer help, but William came to us begging our help about his hands saying he cannot scribe now

2nd spirit I put curse on him after my goodly wife and daughter we so cruel taken and so ill used by them, so you are of our way then lass thalamus is right you do resemble the mother

What year be this?

Why its 1652 lass why do you ask this? For me, its 1987 now how be thee that you can pass through time like this? I know magic very well lass, but I cannot do that. I have the power of bilocation so can be in two places at the same time and speak in both. The Gods take care of me.

As they art of the way you canst bring William here I wishes to speak to him.

Thou art best not doing so again thus night for he may bring them with him canst thou not summon him

1st spirit yes, we can but why would we wish to he did not become the justice here thalamus did and has proved to be a good one demanding evidence of confession witnesses and that it all be entered no matter how trivial it be.

Well, my thinking on this if you were to forgive him and maybe untwist his hands so he may work then maybe it rights a wrong in your time

1st spirit nay wench I cannot my wife and child were both put the torture they broke my child's feet with hammers ripped out her hair and broke her hands but then they dragged her body into a place and hung the poor girl till she could not breathe once able they hung her again, she was but 7 years old how can I u harm him wouldst thee not harm one who kills thine own.

Of course, I would then why thee ask me to do the thing that I cannot it is an eye for an eye. I will not say ought to that man nor help him.

Thalamus canst thou help William does thou understand that without the forgiveness he is trapped wandering time without passing on to a new life. He died alone in that cellar where thy family were held.

Whispers of the Witch by NanyWytch

I cannot lady but maybe thou canst do so can thy work your magic in our time?

Yes, I was living then till 1645 anyway when our people were all drowned then hung as witches

So, if we fetch him you canst do it yes I will help him so he can pass through the light you can watch as this is your home

He is here 1st spirit opens the door come thee hence this lady wishes to speak with thee

William stood there looking so afraid he said I did not mean for your families to be tortured or hung the witch finder said he would use his tools on me if I did not help him, I was so jealous of you becoming the justice instead of me I just thought why not but they went to gather whole families saying thou canst not be a witch alone

Yes, William we are aware of how they work to take lands and wealth, now listen to me I dost hereby forgive thee of thy wrong doings for you have admitted it to both of thy neighbour's thus night hence forth wilt thou not be trouble by pain. Now William come hither to me let me touch they hands

William came I touched him hands till they undid his body smoothed out he was smiling now William can you see that light over their I need you to walk into it then you will be free

Thank you, lady I knows not your name I, be Ashna a friend of thalamus and John

He then was gone

But the house suddenly reverts to 1652 I see thalamus crying he has the baby she us dead he burns her body in the fire, I says why did you burn her so she will not be fed to the dogs as feed they are now hanging people then feeding the bodies to the hunting dogs of the bishop on his lands as the graveyard and beyond are full of good people, they hath destroyed

Lady look into the fireplace there is a tin put your hand up feel for a shelf near the front it will be there help you understand.

Then we heard the soldiers boots again this time we saw men dressed as soldiers and they banged on the door loudly then burst it open, they trod on the floors, searched the house and went out to the well out back as well as rampage through my things.

Harbouring witches is a crime against the church and heresy. William said he used magic to contort my hands so saying that my lying mouth shall seize up and twist as my hands now do.

Where be thy evidence, thou said they have here?

they have poppets they use for magic and they used a poppet against me?

Where be they? I have no knowledge of how witched hide things I am not a witch but a mere scribe of the justice.

So, thou hast been here before yes, many times but only to go to the court we would walk together. Then William Samuel thou know if no evidence be found to say Thalamus be a witch you will have committed a greater crime.

I know Sirs I swear on my life he is a witch.

Then we will question him, who bet that wench there? I have no knowledge of another woman dwelling here maybe she be a witch too.

Whispers of the Witch by NanyWytch

thou art already on shaky ground my men have searched this place found no poppets, nothing that says he is a witch and there be no one else here this night saves the comely wench there.

William stops, I implore you to stop these wild accusations you have killed my Sarah and you will n ow kill me and the innocent sick lad over there from thy jealousy thou were not chosen as a justice

. What be this? he was not chosen as justice then suddenly he sees witchcraft here in my home my Sarah was took a goodly woman who harmed nothing or no one herself yet you hung her yesterday without a trial.

Your Sarah confessed to being a witch hence she was hung.

Anyone will confess under torture as you know.

True but if they be witches, we are being prudent in our finding them early before too much has been done in this village justice, I do know thou has been a good justice since they appointment is it true that you let William go last evening prior to my men coming here

. It is so I did not require his service anymore as the court has a scribe I can use.

Dust thou think then that he is false saying of thee

I do indeed sir.

Then we will come back on the morrow to seek answers in daylight Sir. So be it best night to thee all,

out he orders the soldiers leave once more. We hear them going up the street again.

Look in the chimney on a shelf there be a box it has things in you may need

. Reg was back. We had a drink and talked about what we had seen and heard we took the metal box from the chimney the box contained a book with writings saying that the family had all be engrained even the sick baby, that they had been tortured and hung without trail even the children.

William was not happy till half the village was languishing beneath the courthouse. The list said indictment   748 – 1652 Elizabeth Hatton confessed was hung charge witchcraft, Sarah Hatton confessed and hung, Jacob Hatton aged 6 hung, Thalamus Hatton hung on the charges of witchcraft. Mathew Hatton aged 14 languished then died in the goal.

There was a drawing of the family in the field at harvest time done in charcoal it was a bit crushed, but I could make out Thalamus and Jonathan

The notes said that Samuel was not made the justice as he could neither scribe nor speak, he died a few months later in a cellar having been charged with false statement making but it was too late to save the family. We went outside and then saw the Roman soldiers again marching up the road there was once a garrison at an old fort not far from here. It seemed that night was when time slipped somehow backwards maybe said the locals it was because a witch came back to the village it awakened the old ghosts and spirits. Or maybe it was because the property had been returned to its keepers. The Dolls house was cleaned it suffered no more the village prospered once again.

Potion called Anaesthesia

Whispers of the Witch by NanyWytch

In 1983 I was pregnant with my third child during this pregnancy I had a few problems due to a drug I was given during my last pregnancy to keep me pregnant without a consultant called Mr Graham I would not have children at all. He lost his wife during her pregnancy so dedicated himself to saving other women. My first two children were born at Airedale hospital in Yorkshire. Now I had different Drs was in Macclesfield hospital, they were not as modern back then as Airedale they still had big wards with lots of beds in them. The staff were lovely. I earned a lot of money doing tarot reading for the staff. When I was 26 weeks gone a child arrived in my room one night, she had blonde wavy hair she looked around 2 years old maybe 3 at the most she was holding hands with a very tall man who said nothing at all, she said hello mummy my name is Athena I am your baby. I said hello to her and she left she visited twice more before I came to 38 weeks, I went into labour on the 20th September 1983 was in strong labour most of the day but then it stopped the next day it started again and I was in labour all day, I had not dilated past 3cm but the baby had moved all the way down the birth canal and was wanting get out, she was pushing hard against the hardly open hole. We were both very distressed by now my contractions were awfully hard ones for long periods. But my body was not playing nice. They had broken my waters earlier in the day they now had put monitors on the baby as well as on me I grabbed a Drs hand said get the child out now I cannot do this anymore. I knew I was dying but she was strong. They rushed us to the lift dressed in the lift they put me to sleep in the lift and took me straight into theatre. I thought it was taking a long time for me to be asleep, when I realised, I was on the ceiling looking down at this body whom I was not sure was me. I zoomed down walked around it, nobody saw me they were cutting me then getting the child out. I saw the surgeon lifting her out of my womb I watched all this from outside the body. The monitor was all flashing making noises the man said we are losing her we are losing her crash cart Then I saw a man appear in the corner in a black robe he was rather good looking I said am I dead? Not yet he said but when the clock strikes 4pm yes. I said so what do I do? You come with me now, he said I take people away. But what if I want to stay, it is not your choice lady but mine. Come we need to go now, but I do not want to leave my baby, she can come too one more is not a problem I just leave one here. Well, I am not sure, come with me we need to do this now. I will die then we do not have time. Yes, we do I can stop it till I am ready leave. Ok I said we will come he said no just you right now not here leave her be she has blood issues and is not detached from her guardians yet. I said guardians you mean those two tall people over there near her. Yes, they will care for her she has not decided if she is staying yet but she is a baby, yes but the soul is older. We left the room went around the hospital he would go to a bed touch them and I would watch them leave the body. They would come with us. They seemed attached to him somehow nobody saw them only us. We walked into one ward and nurse dropped the tray she carried I laughed the man said oh that happens a lot here. Hundreds a day are collected at hospitals if they do not come with me, they just remain here. I leave them. we collected people from nearly all the wards a lot from one ward where older people were. A woman yelled out is it my time now? He said Lisa not yet go back to sleep now. She fell back asleep at his touch. Next second, we were outside we were on a bridge, it was like an arched bridge a very bright light was at the other side he said to me take these over their hand them over to those men in the different colour robes. but walk back Do NOT step off the bridge. I said why? Because then we cannot go back. Right, I said but why am I staying when they are not, because I need to show you something as you are fretting about the girls. Yes, I said what will happen to them without us.? He said look over here I looked, and I saw them in west park playing with their dad playing some game. They were laughing and happy again. He said they will be fine they have their dad. Yeah, ok I said can we go get the baby now? Yes, come on he said we do not have much time less than a minute we were suddenly back in the room we just melted through walls. I watched the line on the screen go long and flat they were adding the pads to my body to jump start me. Charged Stand clear the body bumped charged Stand clear again it bumped Bodies do not work without a driver. He said to me ok I am asking you to do you want to go back I said yes, and the child then get back into the body you have 20 seconds before your pronounced dead. I slid back into my body and melted right inside. The machine beeped up and my heart rate was back everything went back to normal after they bumped me twice, I had the burn marks on my body for a while. However, my daughter needed 6 blood transfusions before she was stable. So, no idea whose she had now. In our family we have a decease that mimics leukaemia but is not that decease. We do not know why it just is. When I was pregnant around 4 months a gypsy came to my house an old lady, she said to me I brought you a gift for the child. I took the velvet bag opened it saw it was an old necklace I said I cannot take this it is far too much she said to me it belongs to Athena. She needs it. I took it after she told me how she came to have it, she said a woman came to her and said this had to be given to my child handed it over then vanished she sought me out all she had was a name and date. It had taken her weeks to find me.

I went into a coma for three weeks I woke up 3 times during that time, once the Drs were talking at the base of the bed saying I may still die to move me so as not to distress the others. They moved me another time I saw my husband crying telling me about our child. Then a third time I sat up asked for the baby said I was starving the nurse went for the Dr giving me the child to hold I felt weird after a few minutes so placed the baby in between my legs then fell back to sleep again for another week. I woke when my girls were singing a song to me over the radio. My room was full of cards and presents. My girls were on my bed singing to me.

Athena is now a mother of her own children she has one girl and two boys she is a lovely person loves owls and other animals, but owls are her

Ritual in the woods

Whispers of the Witch by NanyWytch

I was going to Dewsbury today but at the station the platform was full of people yet everywhere really packed I went one man stood out it was as if a light was above him or something I got this creeped out feeling inside me I did t like him not one bit, he worried me why I wasn't sure but he was beautiful so very lovely dark hair that was long and curly he was tall and well his bum was cute his jeans skimmed his body and his dark sweater clung to the muscles but his face was pale, he had blue eyes I felt I knew who he was as I kept being given a name but I sort of said to spirit no way. When the train arrived, we got on from opposite ends of the train, but I got the last window seat and he sat down next to me. I was reading a book about the dark side of the tree; I liked this book had just bought it. I had read several chapters before he trains. He pointed to the book do you know what this is I said yes why are you asking me? Because I am, he touched my leg I moved his hand said don't do that he put his hand back on my leg slid it slowly up my leg I stopped him saying get off me he said you liked it I replied maybe but that is not the point is it you do not have my consent to touch me. He then tried offer me a watch I said no way I do not do time. Then he offered me a gold chain I said look mate I do not know you I do not want any gifts so stop it. Suddenly I felt a needle prick on my leg, my head went woozy I felt odd like I was drugged or something I told myself I was a witch and could override anything I kept telling myself this then sat up and said this is my station he looked at me very odd followed me to the doors said I can come with you I said you're not invited they won't let you in. well he said beautiful lady I will see you again I told Richard about this experience he said that we are tested 3 times during our incarnation to see if we will go to the dark. That is Satan's job he is the tester. He will try awfully hard to get you to go over to the dark. So, this is where the Church gets it from sort of says Richard. But we are going to the woods to meet people for a ritual. Its time I had an acolyte to pass on my craft. So today is about my choice.

Whispers of the Witch by NanyWytch

At the woods which by the way I simply admire so much, the smells the feel of grass under naked feet, the sheer magnificent creations emerging here with all the nature spirits I am truly alive here. There were many men waiting for us, no females except me I heard comments like he brought that witch with him.

I sat down on the earth drawing Sigel on it, a man sat next to me we played a game with geometric Sigel he was countering mine it was good. Then Richard said it was time whilst I had played this game, they had built a fire and a platform with a seat on it an altar and were now ready Richard said to me go sit on that seat as queen of this rite. Replying I said but I does not feel like a queen today and I certainly do not want bless people. Richard said sit down right now stop being petulant.

I sat there thinking of these men they were all magicians not witches. Their way was demand things command spirits served them. Our way is far better we request they help us do something we never try force something. Nature is truly remarkable when you work with it rather than against it.

I saw selfishness, greed, avarice, and people who would stoop to any level to get their own desires. Richard was highly respected amongst them as he was now a real mage. The highest on his path, yet they did not know him how I did. Him I would trust with my very soul often did. He I loved as my brother, friend, teacher.

They invoked the gods my goddess came into me overshadowing my body, talking to me at the same time. I knew he had seen how the goddess was there I could see his eyes feel it in his body, she knew I also did grasp some aspects about the magicians' path I do not know what they can see during rites. When circles are cast I see blue light coming off the sword like that fire of brandy on the pudding. Richard kneels before us hands over the sword, a little knowledge here is the sword represented the power of the circle and rite. So, he had given over the power to my lady. He asked her to bless the participants of the ritual. She declined saying she found them unworthy. Richard said then throw the crown into the fire, the goddess looked at him saying you my friend gave me this sword if you want it back then take it. She knew he would not, because she knew he had respect for her after all he was himself sworn to Isis.

Richard did the rite without the sword, smiling to himself as he looked at us sitting there. My lady told me she did not wish to bless people who kiss arse to get their desires. She does not mince her words. She says it like it is.

After the rite I wandered about the woods collecting herbs and some flowers for the altar. I still had the crown of flowers they had placed on my head. Richard said stay on the path there are mine shafts here. As we walked back to the carpark, I heard comments made to Richard like

If she were my student I would pull in the leash, she would not speak to me that way it is what you get for having a mere witch as a student.

Another comment was why on earth would you wish to teach a mere witch high magic's they do not understand it. They just play about with nature spirits nothing bigger.

Another was she needs putting in her place playing with geomancy when she is a mere witch. She has no idea of its power.

I got the distinct impression I was disliked because I was female and a witch, maybe they were jealous because Richard spent a lot of his spare time with me. Teaching me his ways whilst I taught him mine.

The goddess said come here I want to show you something let us hope your magi can see this. We came to a stream the goddess placed her hand in the water said watch. I looked I saw that later in the day the latter part of the rite would be done, she said can you see into their intent. I said yes jealousy of me that is why the bitter words are cast at me. Yes, she said I do not want to you to be part of later I want you to tell him I need you for something and come unto me. I do not want you harmed by these people.

Richard called out to me do not mess about in the woods today we have things to do he came to me sitting on the earth with my herbs and flowers. Said what are you going to do with these elementals I said nothing why, he said do not take them into my home they can run wild. Really I said laughing I know they are funny little things they mean well though. Agreed said now come and do not permit them to intimidate you. What elementals, no silly men. It is not my business what you choose to do today is not it indeed it was your business in circle. Yeah, but my lady told me to say that as you very well know.

I recall, when I had not long met him, he said to me cast a circle for me then I will watch from here he had sat in a chair at the far side of his room. I set up the altar and I began I was extremely nervous I was not sure it would be powerful enough. But as I was doing it Richard jumped inside saying do not shut me out.

Back at the house they all went into the lounge to sit down moving more chairs into it. I went to the willow tree gave it the crown, asked it to take care of it for the Goddesses. I then took flowers to the altar upstairs, herbs in the kitchen. Finally, I walked into the lounge Richard says acolytes make the tea, others just looked toward me I took orders for tea and coffee, went to make them bring it back I served them. As I got to one who had bad mouthed me I said enjoy I put henbane in it to give it some pep. Another I said well yours I thought belladonna a nice choice enjoy the next now for you it us incredibly special mandrake root just enough not too much be careful it has a bit of a bite. I may have been a little heavy with it but enjoy it. They did not drink it only Richard did. He whispered to me you passed go upstairs now do your own stuff. I need deal with this. Thanks I said leaving one of the men said oh is the little witch not joining us Richard replied no she is busy with her craft don't think she's not known she is a very powerful very cunning witch I have known longer than I have indeed known most of you. I went upstairs out of the way, later he taught me about demons. Said he would take me to meet a man possessed by one. On the morrow we got up early and went to a house in Pontefract. Just a normal looking terraced house Richard said to me no matter what happens do not treat it as odd. I have been working with Mathew for a while now. He made an unbelievably bad judgement one day by inviting a demon to loan his body. Wow I said.

When we went inside the chairs were all upside down, this man who indeed was not Mathew at the time as Richard said where is Mathew today then? The demon replies no idea he is simply not here. You have to talk to me today. He said do sit down, who is this young creature you bring with you? Oh, my student Kathy. Welcome to the mad House I have been remarkably busy painting last night I wanted show you what my world looks like so I painted the entire cellar. OK say Richard are we going to get to see this then? Of course, do follow me and be careful the stairs are tricky. I wondered why this demon seemed so friendly towards Richard.

We went down into the cellar the whole place was covered in pictures of angels and demons fighting but my god these painting was so beautiful even the ceiling was painted with purple blues red sky, he said this is me pointing to one of the picture Richard said and your name is, not important, Richard spoke to him in Latin he replied in Latin.

I have never ever in my life seen paintings like this room. The demon said oh how rude Mathew baked cakes for today talked about coffee. We went back to the lounge he clicked his fingers and the furniture moved itself. He said to me would you like to go make the coffee or do you trust me to bring you some. I said I do not mind it is up to you in that case we will do it my way. The table appeared to just grow cake and coffee I was really liking this demon. We ate cake and drank this lovely coffee chatted it said it had been practicing being human. He claimed Mathew did not mind sharing the body after all it was by invitation which technically meant Mathew was not possessed. It was simply an agreement made therefore it was merging of two different entities into one body. Such a shame Mathew has an aversion to being here today.

Richard later explained about transmutation and transfiguration what Mathew had done could not be undone. Each time he visited he never knew whom would answer the door.

Hekomya.

Means Ray of God, a demon with the power over those who try to oppress, he is a crown of 3 heads, gives victory in battles. Has power over women. He was also so particularly good looking. Tall around 6' 5in blonde cascading hair, brightest blue eyes I has seen. With a torso to dream of.

Whispers of the Witch by NanyWytch

We had gone for a visit to see Richard with the girls, when he came visit us, he had said that Mike and I were unbalanced as I was such a well powered witch carried powers from before with me. That as Mike was a newer soul he was not as strong a male force that I needed in magic's. That he proposed do something about this with mike. They vanished upstairs to the temple room, we went out to the delight of the garden, we played games sang songs, told stories of witches and fairies. Generally had fun outside his garden was so nice having an old gatepost like a Goddess many trees flowers herbs plus this beautiful willow tree. Tanith said it was like wind in the willows. She was told that these books lived on the stairs. When we were going in for lunch. Overheard Richard say never let her see that Sigel, or name if you do, she can call him. She is a very cunning experienced witch so watch out. As we were eating I sat across my husband and kissed him passionately at the same I took the paper from his shirt pocket then after seeing it placed it back without stopping kissing. Too late remarks Richard I told you she cunning. Back home we meditated each night one of the nights I waited till I saw Mike leave his body then called Hekomya, who came I spoke to him asked if he could help me get a boy child this time. He said if you like kiss me, I did he kissed so differently than my husband. How could this be it was my husband's lips.

He said make love tonight immediately after I am not visible I will help you, so I began to wake mike up we made love readily and eagerly I never mentioned having called the demons help. The love making felt different more passionate more intense it made me question who I was having sex with. But it was mikes body mikes lips, so I pushed the idea away.

A few months passed I am with child again, but I held out till I was sure the child was going to thrive inside me once I reached 26 weeks I was sure we were past the dangers of losing another baby.

Whispers of the Witch by NanyWytch

One night as I was sleeping something near my door woke me, I saw a shadow of a tall person holding the hand of a small blonde-haired boy around just two years old no more. The boy stood half shadowed by the dark

he said are you a mother? Yes why? Then do you like boys? Yes, I replied then why do you not have any? Mine died before they were born sweet child. Well, they tell, me I must find a mother now, that I has to be born again. Will you really love me? Of course, why do you ask?

Well mothers do not like me they do bad things, like what come into the light so I can see you. I cannot you will not want me then, come into the light he glanced to the tall angel guarding Him it nodded. He steps forward that's when I saw him his poor small body was covered in water burn all down his back and neck face. I said who did this to you! My mother did it she put boiling water on me to kill me said I was a demon. I died that day I was 2 years 4 months old I had not really had my life. That is why they say I must be born again as my life was cut short.

What is your name? I am called Damien, but my magical name is Mythrynn I will come to you on the 13th August at midnight 1985 I will be born in the dark moon when the planets are aligned. With this he was gone.

Whispers of the Witch by NanyWytch

I did go into labour on the 12th, but it stopped. Then in the afternoon of the 13th I went into labour; however, the same thing occurred my body did not permit my cervix to dilate past the 3 cm mark a huge difference from 10cm. Again, the child moved down the birth canal, head pressing against my cervix wishing to be born. The consultants said right take her to theatre it was now 11.30pm. On Friday 13th August if he was right, he had to be born in 30 minutes time.

When I woke up, they handed me a picture of my baby boy I took one look and said hello Damien your here. He was perfect such a good baby hardly cried unless hungry.

On the 3rd day after the birth I was rather weepy, but in the afternoon the whole coven appeared in the hall outside the ward with staff's sword and gifts. The nurse said let them in now draw your curtains. The staff knew I was a witch after all I had been making money giving them readings at £20 a time. Often Drs would come just to chat about herbs and things to help healing. As the day wore on these odd stories were spreading around the hospital,

There is this witch she gave birth to a boy at midnight on Friday 13th in the dark moon. He must be the devil's child.

Later on, it had changed again,

This witch has had a boy at midnight who is a demon, for sure he must be evil as he came on Friday 13th after all witches are evil are, they are not.

The next story was that witch had a child named Damien, in the dark moon he has no soul he is the devil's own you know he will tell havoc everywhere. Witches came lots of then They did a ritual around his bed welcome the devil.

The last version was the worst

That witch in the other room born a devil child without a soul it's going to infest everyone by the devil and bring hell here to our world we must kill it it's not holly we must kill her as well as we cannot claim to belong to God and do nothing when evil comes right before our own eyes These stories just got worse as the day went on when the truth was, I was just like them had given birth to my son was recovering. Come shift change I had gone for a bath leaving Damien sleeping in his bed at the side of mine he was due feeding at 10pm. I had this lovely long bath my clips had been removed and they gave me something put into the water help heal me. When I returned to my bed I nearly burst a blood vessel the sight meeting my eyes was horrendous. My bed had these pieces of paper with black crucifix drawn on them, one on my pillow another on my quilt, more above my bed but worse than this one on top of my baby's body taped to him one on his cot and above his head hanging there was a real wooden crucifix. I turned about addressing the other 3 mothers who were colluding together I said whom did this? They shrugged their shoulders we do not know; I was so upset anger was brewing very well inside me thus was outrageous it was an insult to me and my beliefs. It was 1985 for god's sake not 1645.

I screamed at them whom did this. L swear if you do not tell, me I will hex you all. So, tell, me now one of them stammered it was the black African sister, giving out the meds in next room. She came in and she put them over your bed and baby muttering she will stop the witch doing anything as her god will not permit it having a demon child it needs to die. She was seriously deranged we are scared please do not hex us please we did not do it. I sat with them a minute I said thank you for telling me do you agree with what she has done one lady called Sarah said no way I am Jewish I could not do that to anyone just because they did not believe in god. I told them we do believe in gods and higher powers. Just not the Christian God.

Tearing down all of them I whispered to my child do not worry love mother will protect you. Going into the nurse's empty station I stuck one to her bag, one to her coat, another on the book she had to write in. Then I stuck 3 upsides down crosses to her window in front of her eyesight.

I sat back down on the chair turned so I could see straight into there, I fed my child and waited. She had started a war, she attacked me, and my child I was entitled to defend myself and the babe in my arms from such nasty minded behaviour. I fully understand how brainwashed some Christians are but the Africans well they are used to voodoo and Dambulla they Add the Christian god to their own and put their whole heart and soul into worship. It is a big thing to dress up and dance sing and pray. So, I understand how she might think she was doing right. However, attacking a powerful witch is never without consequences natural law states you create a cause, and the effect comes after it did me.

She walks into her office sees the upside-down crosses on one I had written

DO NOT FUCK WITH ME BITCH I ALWAYS WIN...

L sat there watching her gazing straight at her, she screamed out the witch cast her evil onto me its crawling on my skin I can feel it. She was screaming so loud a Dr ran into the room. He saw her flailing about trying to kill imaginary demons she said were attacking her. She claimed that child should be killed he will spread evil across the world you must stop him. She is attacking me. The Dr looked at me sitting on the chair with my baby then called psyche ward come fetch this sister. She screamed the place down they had to fasten her down, inject her to stop her swearing that demons were eating her very soul.

The Dr's came to me saying what happened here. I explained about the papers she had covered my bed in the other mothers said she did it as soon as she came onto the ward, she was acting crazy, she kept saying the child must be killed.

Then in breezed Beryl one of my coven along with our main male witch Marlin this place is humming. What have you done here; I laughed its only magic?

Anyway, babes we are here now, can I hold him say hello, of course Damien was very alert for a new-born. He watched her gazing straight at her I think he knew they were here to protect him. That night we watched the Omen, then Wicca man. Ate cakes drank wine generally had fun I allowed beryl take care of Damien till morning so I could get a full night's rest.

Time moves on fast when you are not watching, it was the wiccaning of my son today Mabon, my daughter Athena's birthday as well. Guests were invited all brought food for the potluck supper. We had rules where people must bring food wine or ale and cakes. They could ask something of the gods providing they offered something to them candles incense flowers silver whatever they liked.

So, everything was prepared I go inside the temple to light the candles and incense. A tall man is standing right near the altar. I say excuse me you need go back to the other guests till we are ready. He turned around in his blue cloak; his beard trimmed his face sort of familiar. A patch over one eye. Then announced you have a guest here called Silver fetch her to me now. I said why? He said just do as your bid child.

I went to Silver said to her this man is in our room demanding you attend him right now. I do not know him, so you need talk to me what is happening here sister.?

Awe I am dead I just know it will be Odin, why! Well, you know those Satanists raped and stabbed my daughter well I asked for vengeance the gods said no. I well I called on the powers of Fenrir they were mauled to death. I said darling you are a bad girl hey bitch not as bad as you, but my darling I am just so beautiful with it. She washed dressed in her robes tied a cord to her Wrist.

Yeah pigs are blue and pink elephant's fly. I escorted her to the temple, as she stepped into the circle my warrior held me back tis the business of the gods he said not yours just listen and watch.

Odin stood tall he yelled at her who do you think you are defying me, I told you no vengeance no blood.

I will not be disobeyed you are my servitor not I yours. You will do no magic's for the next six moons this rite will be your last for that time I am removing your power to read runes. So, you learn we the gods do not take disobedience lightly. She tried to protest he slapped her hard she flew towards us I broke free from my warrior's grasp stepped into the circle. Saying I do not care whom you are this is my home I will not have violence here

STEP away It is not your business child. Step away I stood there said no its heathen law I must treat you well as my guest, but it is my home, so it is my rules.

He laughed she said you were a spirited creature, whom I asked? You lady it is a rule amongst the gods, that should another god wish to enter another's Hall or room he needs the consent of that god to enter. I asked your ladies consent to be in her space. Now if you are not offended I am of the mind to stay for your rites. I will bring suitable gifts. Am I permitted I nodded of course no question. He was gone.

This was how my life was the Gods just dropped in when they felt like it, to tell me something or to simply be for a time they taught me a lot, having Diana as my Goddess I was not a weak woman I was very good at archery had a great teacher. Odin was more a warrior than anything he said it is better to stand and fight than die on your knees, to live well die soon rather than live an empty life.

Whispers of the Witch by NanyWytch

He taught me about all the others, the nine worlds he loved tell stories and poems were a favourite. But mead and ale were more so when he came, he always brought mead we laughed and danced sung. Times were incredibly good for us now.

The ritual went on without a hitch Odin put a Thors hammer on the altar said for the boy. The party went on into the early hours. We really did welcome our son

When Damien was around 6 months old in town the girls wanted go to the cafe inside St Michael's Church. So, we said yes took Damien from his pram I carried him but as soon as we were through those doors, he started to bite kick scream the place down he was wriggling about like he had fleas in his draws. As soon as we went through the side door he calmed back down. He sat in the highchair good as gold I said to Mike what on earth was all that, maybe its connected to what was done to him last time maybe they were religious. Damien ate and drank the girls had their ice cream and flakes their coke went the loo, then it was time go back through the main body of the church as soon as we did the kicking and screaming began again once outside it was as if nothing had happened. We laughed saying well maybe we ought to use another cafe next time Mike said maybe we have a demon for a son which is funny because if you ask Damien, he will say he is., when he was around 2 his sisters were quite mean to him, they would draw 666 on his head in felt pen tell him he was a demon's child. Damien would run to me saying they did it again mummy I not demon. I said of course not darling you will, always be my sun king. He would go away happy but later he would get his sisters back when he had the A team, he cut off their heads buried them in garden when asked why he replied they died in a war. Ok then he started placing his action men astride his sister's Barbie's Athena would say he is making it like his action men are seeing my Barbie's mum tells him stop it. I would laugh.   Prior to this private wiccaning we held a more public one at the Ankh centre a place run by some friends where we had attended

This was offensive. She attacked my Baby.

Paper crucifixes placed on my bed but also taped to babies blanket and cot. As a mother I was really upset

many rituals or workshops, we would meet the same people all the time so I had felt others should be able take part in a ritual with us at this lovely place. We did not give out his magical name obviously then as he was just a month old. They were disappointed at the fact we did not want to give it out, but you see I protected my children when around magic very well. They were permitted attend Rites, allowed at the parties after rituals most of the time they would wake up just at the right moment knock on the temple door Tanith would say can we come inside now. Later on, the night of the private wiccaning at our home it had been a good day but later on something occurred I am still unsure as to how or why. People had given us gifts we had placed them on the table so our guests to see them one gift was a picture of a forest painted over the glass of a mirror in a frame we liked the forest I had said that you can actually walk into that wood. But if you do you must be aware of the wolves hiding there.

I had gone for a rest I needed feed my baby so took him with me went lay down I had taken Damien with me high on the astral because I had been warned something was not right in the lounge. My guides showed me some pictures of events unfolding in there with John one of my recent open circle members. I had no idea that alcohol turned him quite violent. He must have drunk a lot of the Ale, mind you we did have a full barrel of that plus a lot of wine available. Most people brought gifts of wine with them. I was shown John with really red eyes, he was fighting with Hekomya near the temple why I had no idea till Silver explained it all later. But I heard a huge crash into the temple door, I saw Silver drag him back away from that door. She knew the Gods were still there, but she was not worried about them but about my warrior guardian she had seen him earlier. The temple door had burst open flown right back against the rear wall where one of our magical mirrors was hung. Then a huge crash again it sounded as if my horseman had arrived I heard his horse snorting his hooves banging the floor like he does when impatient. Silver said the temple door opened slowly behind it was the dark warrior sword drawn. Silver said she made up a sort of mental story of what had just happened the warrior looked at her nodded then slowly closed the door, but she knew he was waiting as she heard the scuffing on the floor of the horse.

I woke up walked down my hall, but it was like I was still not wholly back from the high astral. I walked past Silver she grabbed me said your horseman is behind the door be careful. I knocked on the door three times said it is me. He replied enter. I went inside my temple looked like it had been destroyed by something as my floor was strewn with glass from one mirror. My warrior said that man outside has violence on his mind. Get him out of the house he is dangerous right now. I said he looked possessed the warrior said no too much drink he cannot control. Himself a shadow has come from somewhere in this house I need to ride around find it. Will it be in John as drink weakens you, he is not yet trained in our ways, so you are telling me he does not know how to ground energies. No but I can send Silver with him she can help ground him. I came out of temple seconds later john fell down the stairs, I does not know if he was pushed or he just stepped back he was still arguing with Hekomya whom wanted him outside. Same as my warrior.

Silver said

John had been drinking ale with others when he was talking to Mike about open circle stuff, then he was seen staring into that picture. It was as if he saw something suddenly a shadow was seen entering him his eyes went deep red, he collapsed on the floor. People in the room were tending to him. He woke up in this frenzy attacking people,

Mike was forced into physically restraining John. I placed my hands on his arms said stop reacting to the rise in psychic energy you are making it worse come outside to ground it. He did not hear me or chose not to. He seemed to have little respect for women. But I had to help, something to do with that picture. Yoshi came out the room asking if he was OK as we had taken away from the other guests. To calm him down but he was trying to fight Mike, who was not letting him go. He got free fell straight into the temple door, it smashed open he fell into the entrance of the room. Backwards, I grabbed him out just as I saw your warrior step from broken mirror. He is enormously powerful I saw the sword unscathed thought holy chap he will take off his head. So, I told your warrior what had gone on. After he went back into your room there was another crash I think your warrior removed the mirror from the wall. We got John outside I helped ground him poor guy was shaking with raw energy it did not help that Carol was wanting walk the dark path Phil had invoked Kali, his dark goddess. So, it took those initiates who were far more skilled sort out the mess. So, Iesha, Reg, Dot, myself and a couple of others helped out. Ashna walked back into lounge took a hammer smashed the mirror picture after removing it from the wall. John collapsed again on the grass outside something like a black shape came out if him. Went straight upwards. Ashna, and the others cleansed the place and it went back to how it was before the picture was unwrapped and hung I wondered whose gift it was then I realised where I had seen that wood that view no wonder poor John the only unprotected person had been attacked. Ash wax very upset about the mess in her temple but the goddess was there to calm her down I held her as she cried letting out the tears, she ought to have cried at the hospital Beryl hugged her too then Richard took her away do a rite for her help her heal. Childbirth takes a lot out of the mother as they go inside themselves to create the life. Then bring it to fruition giving of themselves al, the time. It takes 9 months make the child 9 months for the mother to regain her strength. The rest of us were now dancing in the lounge.

We did not retire till dawn next day the children had not gone to sleep till midnight so the next day was spent chilling out we took the children to the park. Whilst others house cleaned sweeping away any magical energy left behind. The house was rebalanced. Dot a Reg went out buy a new mirror for the temple we painted it with moons stars.

Chalk and board rubber.

I venture to mention high school, we were a large extended family with those who had gone this school before. Ever thought that teachers would measure you by your distant cousins' level. Well Hen bury High do they place you in these boxes, cry when you step off or out of the parameters they set.

High School meant growing up, choosing subjects, boys, in fact I worried about what others might think silly. When do you tell a boy you are a witch? Do you tell them like this? On the first date, oh by the way I am a witch and so is the family. Or do you wait till it gets past the kissing stage then say you do know that I am a fully-fledged witch. In my mind they ran a mile at the word witch.

Making your own choices. They insisted I a pagan attend a Christian hymn singing praying 30-minute morning thing, all for 5 minutes at the end when the head talked about shit. I was supposed to stand there and take part in something I did not belong to, no thanks I would stroll in late on purpose to miss it because let us be real here the Muslims, Jews, Sikhs didn't go they were excused what but not pagans.

Their next famous statement was we do not do religious education here but comparative religions. Such a crock of shit, they did Christianity versus Muslims, Christianity versus Jews, Christianity versus all other beliefs of any kind because we have the only true God, we are 100% correct. Everyone else are heretical arseholes & devil worshippers.

We did one half lesson on Hinduism they proved they knew nothing about it. The Jewish part was simple we ignored it all because Christians do not come from Jews, they have a different bible. They did not cover our beliefs Witchcraft so when the teacher said now, we have covered what we need we will return to my favourite religion Christianity. I stood up said

Sir, you have not done mine,

pray tell me Tanith what is that? He said staring over his spectacles at me with this look of pure disdain.

Well Sir we are Wyci, it means we are witches and pagans. He gasped in sheer shock rubbing his chin almost losing control of the class who all yelled yea Tanith. So, we discussed Witchcraft, the result being I took questions home to my mother. Couple of weeks later we were back on guess what Christianity, but the sacrificed god syndrome kept getting stuck in your hands and feet not to mention the neck. There we were 32 kids of 15 years old bored senseless whilst he drones on and on about the crucifixion of Jesus.

Now earlier you heard about the telekinesis well I had grown and so had its I was good at it now could do it easy. So, what is a girl to do to pass the last hour of the lesson as I tried awfully hard to not hear. On a wet dreary Wednesday afternoon two full one-hour periods of this shit, we know the Jews killed him. We know it was horrible but where is the proof he came back from the dead. Oh yeah none.

Has anyone come back who dies I do not think so? Our gods are not dead, so they drop in all the time. Experimentation is what of course could I do it was the question. I was going to practice some of my mental skills to amuse me and prevent sleep.

The teacher had just put down half a piece of chalk for another new piece, so I concentrates on that piece of chalk whilst doodling on my book I wrote my name is Bethany I am here.

As I concentrated the chalk floats unto the board and writes the same on it. I then write talk to me some of the students start talking about it just appearing on the board. If I stopped the chalk dropped to the floor so I picked the board rubber smeared it across the board. The teacher turns about says what is all this noise when you should be writing all this down. As soon as he turned again I wrote talk to me now holding the chalk floating in the air. A girl screams I drop the chalk. I do sweep the board with the board rubber wiping it he sees this empties the class its haunted or possessed by the devil. He had to fetch the visiting priest to well no idea what he could do the evidence was no longer there.

We were stood in the corridor and I just had to do it after all I was bored this was fun. I made the chalk write on the board come and find me, they had not a clue what was doing this or whom or how. They are so closed minded it was easy mess with them. They declared we would need go home early because well we could not go in there our souls could be affected.

Some of the girls who hated me told the priest I was a witch and I did it. The priest almost crapped his dress right there. God preserve us from this chaos heaven knows what effect this will have on the school. What does it mean witches in s catholic school no it must not be, it simply cannot be permitted? We simply cannot condone this type of child amongst us she could affect all the children with her wickedness. She must be converted to the Christian beliefs quickly to save her very soul. It is our duty we must save her from the devil himself who already has a firm grip. They sent me home with a letter to my parents that I could not return to school unless I was baptized into their faith. My mother said I was baptized in the church of England not the Catholic faith. She told them she did not see the point in having a baby then trying drown it in the font with water from the kettle. The priest threw a fit he went blue and purple with rage. When my mother said so can I have it in writing that you are expelling my daughter on religious grounds because she is not Catholic. Shame it will mean all the other non-Catholic children will need the same letter, so that is some let us some 60% of pupils for which you receive money to educate.

Now re I suggest you re admit my daughter unless you can prove beyond a doubt that her being pagan has adversely and detrimentally affected this school. I do not mean your opinions or beliefs but the law because I will sue. Its discrimination against my child's freedom of thought and beliefs.

Evidence suggests that Glenworth Manor Estate was once the property of the knights Templars. Passing to the knights of St John in 1312.

In 1301 it was found to be held by Abbott Fountain and Roger Mow bury as two calculate in Glenworth for $1/8^{th}$ of a knight's fee which is £4 per year as a knight's yearly fee was £32

Guidance is often given in dreams as well as teachings I was told I needed travel to Gainsborough to the village of Glenworth that the Manor was in ruins having been burnt down by owner years before. The only part left was the old stable block now turned into four large cottages.

A friend of ours had died a friend who made the most exquisite jewellery you could ever desire. He had been doing some kind of dark magic gone mad killed his family and himself. Why we may never know. So many pagans travelled to this small village for the funeral. A friend of mine named Cathy lived in one of the cottages with her husband and son called Seth. She suggested we stayed with her, which we were to do. As we drove into this old village it was rather odd, there was the new houses a shop at one side of the green but then it seemed divided away from the older pagan side of the village. As we drove, we hit what seemed some type of invisible barrier that felt like moving through jelly. Then once outside it the village appeared to be old.

It is said that the knights Templars worshipped Baphomet as well as God, but we do not know the truth of this.

Whispers of the Witch by NanyWytch

My memory of this village came from the realm of Charles 2nd the Lord and lady of the manor were pagans and led the villagers this way no church was on thus land till the year 1846.

Cromwell men raided this village finding them to be witches cut off their hands and feet believing they could not do magic or enter heaven with parts of the body missing I was at that time hung from a tree.

The manor had a secret door via a stained-glass window to the cellars below the manor where an incredibly old temple was found. There was also an escape tunnel that came into the attic of one of the old cottages.

Because the plague had wiped out a lot of the villagers, at night you would see four men in plague masks with webbed things over there boots walk a Cross the field, when I saw them at dusk I said why are they dressed like that Cathy said it happens every night here they are not living we think they are spirits. The wood had other issues it was all male trees stagnate pool in the middle walked here the roots of trees grabbed your legs. Cathy and I were going to plant flowers and female trees to balance it back up as we did so we heard the trees whispering

The witches have come back the witches are here,

Cathy took me to the edge of the village to the one roomed schoolhouse, 2 women were in there wearing 13th century clothing, they said the school is closed today. Cathy introduced me as another witch, these women took my hands oh my goodness you are all coming back we so missed you. The village is not the same without you. Then they were simply gone. Cathy said since she had been here just a few weeks she has been seeing a lot of really odd things. She said the village is cut off from the new part by a barrier it is as if its stuck in time somehow.

At this time quite a few witches were having the same dream it was as if we were all given one part of a jigsaw to be placed back together. It is said that when a coven left a place the artefacts and knowledge was divided amongst them so not one person held onto all of it. In the hope some lived past the burning times.

Now you all know how the sun sets slowly and the dark gradually comes over the sky not in Glenworth one minute it was light another minute it was dark but that is when all the odd stuff began. Cathy said we need light the fires and candles stay together; do not go outside in the dark you may not come back. I asked why she said at night here lots of odd things occurred like trees having the shapes of a person as if they were once a person who was trapped inside a tree. That children wandered the village who were not living.

That night we were to sleep on airbeds in the two living rooms the girls in one myself and mike in another. We were near the old kitchen which was just a Belfast sink and drainer a few cupboards most food was in the old pantry in the cellar. Well around 3am I woke up because I could hear water, I got up running my eyes to see children in the kitchen running the water and splashing about happily as if they hadn't seen water inside a house I watched them when they saw me, they turned they were plague children.

We decided to go check out if the temple still existed as we had both been killed in 1645 for being witches. We knew a lot about the village we had no idea how as neither of us had set foot here since 1645. So, we began in the first cottage as it was empty, the person owning the ruined Manor lived in middle two. We went to the attic moved a wooden bookcase which we knew moved it slid sideways if as you pressed a shelf. We walked inside the walls down the steps full of cobwebs with torches this tunnel was made of stone. It was cut out of the rocks. We saw a large boulder blocking the path ahead for a moment we thought we could not get past, but it moved when touched like it knew we were witches. I have no idea what we expected to find but at the end of the tunnel was a round shaped room with just fruit boxes on the floor but markings under the dirt forming a beautiful circle the tiled floor had our god and goddess entwined in ivy. Much of it now broken we had brought candles incense wine cake and a cloth. We intended do a ritual to heal the village.

We set up four quarter lights used the fruit boxes as an altar with wine and cake, using just our athame we cast the circle and then did the right to heal the village we both seemed to know exactly what to do and say. We asked the gods for help were told we had to find the four seals at the edge of the village and break them before returning to the earth. That once this was done the village would be healed things would grow because the goddess would come back. Everything would be made right,

So, we drank wine ate cake enjoyed sitting in this sacred space where our gods were worshipped so long ago. We hoped this would work but both of us were curious to see if the other entrance through the mirror was there. Maybe that part of it was destroyed when the manor burnt down. But we found the old stone steps walked up them hoping we were right we lifted the metal catch and it opened we stepped onto the bottom of the old staircase. It was a mess we decided it was not safe to go this way so went back the way we came making sure it was all closed down sealed and left. We went around the village seeking these seals we must have seemed mad digging in the soil at the quarters of the village we found these clay Sigel's drawn into the clay very impressive talisman we broke them and returned each one it was as if we had lifted a curtain of darkness enveloping that village all we could hear was the witches are back the witches are here. It was as if that whisper ran through the elements and then we went to where the barriers were nothing they had gone; we had done it undone magic done in the 1600s.

Just by being led by our dreams.

I loved that village year was 1982

DEMO'RAI.

A word about demons, all demons were once angels because God sent 300 of his best to earth to destroy humans these angels decided not to obey but instead teach these beings about art, science, maths, physics, writing, languages, even singing. Without this knowledge they gave us we would be simply ignorant vessels.

Demons do not need a body to exist they are omnipotent also hermaphrodite. Sometimes they do however possess a human, but it normally takes a while.

I had been in the coven now nearly 3 years I had passed through much of the knowledge and often was leader of the rites. However, the coven had really changed when the high priest and high priestess split up half of it going with her half remaining. Our half ran by the high priest who began his life in the church before being defrocked by them for studying witchcraft.

He wore his cassock as his robe they make great robes as they have pockets. I have one because I am permitted to be addressed as right reverend. However much preferring priestess. On this day I was travelling to Manchester to the full moon esbat.

At the station in Leeds, I got on the train it was not a through train but an older type with separate carriages. Only 3 people were in it as well as myself we set off as we came out of a long dark tunnel a man was sitting opposite me. I wondered where he had boarded the train as we had not stopped at all,

Whispers of the Witch by NanyWytch

He said listen to me carefully your life depends on it, they mean to cause you great harm. The old ambulance will be there when you arrive. Do not eat cake, do not drink the wine. Refuse it today make your own drink have tea. I will be there to help but you MUST, and this is especially important, cast the circle your way use your goddess no, matter what happens know we will, be there to help you.

This really worried me should I turn back go home he said no you cannot face this head on be brave it will be ok.

I remembered Richard telling me that any magician worth his salt would want to bind me by demon. Because of my powers of bi-location and other powers I carried over from previous lives.

I was used to spirits, angels, demons, gods dropping into my life. It was normal for me. As he said it was there the old ambulance travel van, decorated nicely but all the same it meant another high priest was there waiting for me not just mine

As I walked in I was offered wine before I had taken off my coat put my bag down, I said no thank you I really need a cuppa right now, but it's your favourite wine we got it specially for you the bulls blood red come on one glass and do try the cake it lemon drizzle you love it we baked it ourselves. No I has eaten at the station. I went to the kitchen made myself tea,

Rick said we have decided go do some ritual practice in fact we are going to try a transmutation ritual. L said a what he said it is simple no worries we will lead all we need you to do is read one paragraph th rest is up to us, you have done overenshadowment before its sort of the same thing. I was very unsure that spirit said they meant to harm me. I knew they had been studying high magic's. Because Rick had done some of it adding it into our coven stuff I still have my original book of shades from 1980 Rick said we will go to lore's place; it is better for this type of magic. I trusted my high priest had no reason not to. So, agreed go and take part, after all it was just a ritual was it not. Once at Lore's place which was an exceptionally large house in its own grounds,

On arrival Lore hands me a big white robe saying you will wear this we will be in red. Then he hands me a piece of paper that said the rite was dedicated to dark Isis, I had not worked with Isis since I lived in ancient Egypt. I said I do not have any affinity with Isis can I use my goddess Lore laughs will not make any difference to the outcome. When we went into this room up three steps I was amazed at the size of the room, it had free standing metal quarter light set up that were very gothic. The altar was in the west not north but what drew my attention was the triangle of art outside the circle to the left it had two lines inside it were Sigel's I did not understand, then salt lots of it. I said what is that for as my only knowledge of them back in the 80s was from films with Christopher Lee in them. Asking what we are using it for they said well you will stand inside it whilst we do the invocation its perfectly safe.

The words kept going through my head they intend do you great harm. I knew now I had to go through with this and trust spirit 100% to take care of me. Before this time I never knew how closely the gods watched over me, I said so what circle are we using then, Rick said ours of course You know it without the book. So can I cast it you do the quarters does not matter to us it does not change the ritual

. We began with the foul shade, then carried on I did our circle they did the four gates we blessed it with salt incense fire oil. It was ready now then Lore opened a gate said you go stand in there it will all, be over soon a little experience for you before tonight.

(Authors note transmutation means to change the form of something. Whereas transfiguration means to change the aspect of to a more elevated character.)

Once in the triangle Rick & Lore did the invocation s, suddenly something entered my body via the crown chakra, then I could not see hear or feel anything I had lost the body it was no longer mine I was just this small ball of light in the head. It was the most terrified I have ever been, then the voice said who are they? I said give me my body back, later it said not now I am busy who are they? It was loud echoing inside my head, why cannot I see or feel or hear! Because child they invoked a powerful demon into you me, now had I entered in full power you would be a pile of Ash on the floor.

Whispers of the Witch by NanyWytch

 These two people have just tried to kill you. However, my boss said I had not to harm you. You have some immensely powerful friends. Now we are going to play my game, who are they! I said Rick is on the left and Lore on the right they are high priests of two different covens Rick being mine. Ok which knife on that altar is yours the horned handled one, now then who cast this circle? I did my what a clever witch you are. Give me my body back now oh shut up whining you are alive are not . Yes, but I wants to see what is happening here. I suppose I could let you see what is going down. Suddenly I was looking down what felt like binoculars to some yellow eyes then I could see

 Lore kneeling holding up the wine, to the demon it took the chalice with my hands, but I could not feel my hand holding it then as it drank I couldn't feel my lips on the cup or it go down my throat. Then they offered cake I said do not eat that. Awe sweet witch have they poisoned it. No idea but spirit told me not eat it.

Awe so these priests whom I last saw in the church cellar years ago have used the very same rite they did to invoke me then I expect they want the same to bind you to me then loan your powers. So little witch what shall we do with them? You cast the circle which means you can open it, your knife we will need it. Now I will give you the front half of the body, the issue might be getting past archangel Michael he does not much care for demons, but I suspect he knows what is going down here. As you were warned earlier.

 Move some of the salt with your foot rub some of the Sigel's out breaking the triangle. Then we will take a nice walk.

we walked out the circle towards the south gate before Michael who was standing some 7ft tall in his warrior clothing he wore red garments and a golden breast plate he was facing us his sword in hand he watched us coming toward him.

The demon then said you have never seen the outside of a circle, have you? Those things that look human once were they are now shades ignore them, the creatures at the bottom are elementals and those darker shades are with me. They are lesser demons or larval entities.

We arrived before Archangel Michael who simply stood aside winking at me, I had never seen him do that before, so the demon was right, they knew and were letting us back into the circle.

Lore dropped the wine; Rick froze against the wall dropping the cake onto the carpet. We walked towards the altar and oops it fell over everything now on the floor, easy laughed the demon. He said to Lore plan B maybe as plan A just failed. What do you want from me I am busy I do not have time wait about for you play stupid games?

Lore knelt and said great being it is just she is so powerful, and we just thought you could give us her powers. He laughed so much it shook my body echoed through me, wine I need wine it shouted bring me wine. Inside my head he said they seem to think you are dead that it worked obviously not that bright. Now you are going to enjoy some wine that we open, then you will kiss Lore on the mouth tongue and all

I will not I say back little witch I have a job to do today you will kiss him if you want the body so drink the wine and then kiss him you will know why once it is done. I did as he said kissed Lore on the mouth with tongue then it felt like I was sucking all his powers from him like hovering him out it was a rather nasty feeling his face told me he knew what was happening the god's justice. The demon said ok it is time to leave I said what about Rick awe he comes later baby witch. We get him into his temple cast circle then you kiss him why because it has to be in sacred space I have taken your body let us see what his plan is. Back in the van they were both arguing Rick saying you did not tell me what this would do to her, you lied to me how do I explain that she is possessed by a demon we invoked into her. Now you are leaving the mess for me clean up.

Back inside I had the body well most of it, I said you have to help me it is killing me please I needs my body I trusted you look what you have done to me. I said we had you go into the temple do a rite he backed off no he said I do not know how I was not that kind of priest, they are different I do not know how. I cannot I said you are coming into the temple if I has drag you there myself you are going to help me. The demon said well I suppose dragging him in works for me. Once in I cast the circle Rick tried to leave but the demon blocked the door, he pulled at the door it did not budge. Ok kiss him now. I did and the same hovering thing happened his face said it all absolute fear wrapped onto it.

Once done the demon said my job is done baby witch. However, we have a problem we are merged it means I am part of you and you part of me now so we can work together. I said I have the body though yeah sometimes I am here to help you prevent this occurring again. That is to be my job I will not interfere unless you are in danger. We can talk though I can help you understand.

The next issue is tonight you do realise he will be in no fit state run a ritual he will hide away for a bit. I think you scared him. Me it was not me I did not do it. You were the one who dragged him into the temple demanded he did stuff.

The only time he has interfered has been if someone tried to harm me otherwise, we just talk.

However occasionally he gets irritated with humans, at my husband's birthday party we were going to several pubs. My gay friend from university was upset his boyfriend had gone to see a girl, another friend of ours. Saying he would meet at the club. Fine by the others around 6 of us at that time, Carl whined his arse off he was really annoying me. This was not about him, the girl Gale had just lost her baby, needed some comfort so Graham said he would go for a while which we thought good of him. Carl did not see it like this, but he could be petty.

The demon said to me can we slap it yet, I said no be good, boring he said. My friends were used to me having conversations with things they could not see. But Carl carried on for two hours just whining about his boyfriend. As we walk out the bar my demon grabbed him held him by the throat little feet not touching the ground said shut the fuck up bitch. Carl went white as a sheet, he put him down when bouncers over the
Road asked if there was a problem, I said not anymore thanks for your concern it is all sorted

Carl looked at me said that was not you as it was not your voice No, I said you met my demon side. Remind me never fall out with you, the rest of the night was simply great fun.

What they did wrong was place an initiated priestess inside the triangle who had cast the circle. It meant she was in charge of it had the power of the sword. The guardians would answer to her not them So she could walk out of the triangle. That is what the demon found the most entertaining error.

Evocation means to bring to manifestation something from another place in our realm. A triangle of art is used by magicians in ceremonial magick as they like to command spirits to obey them. Whereas witches do not command something they ask it. There is a huge difference.

Whispers of the Witch by NanyWytch

Hollow Whispers

188 copyright Ashna Yates BSC 2020

Whispers of the Witch by NanyWytch

. You do not seriously expect us to live their mother says my teenage daughter when we went to view a house. After the bridge but before the river the dream kept saying when we went to get the keys standing over the other side of the road I realised it was the house I had seen the Victorian children at the window. I do darling a bit of paint will do wonders to it they are going fix it up after we move in. Come on let us look, OK but I am having the biggest bedroom. Yeah, OK love, we entered the house it was well incredibly old, very dirty and the hall was thus horrible treacle brown colour I fact all the doors were treacle brown. We went to the back room which was huge with open fireplace I loved open fires they made it homely and cosy. The kitchen was a pink bit of worktop and a sink. The garden was nice big with an old square patio, but those roses had to go we both hated them. Tanith had run upstairs I walked up slowly thinking about colours and furniture but four steps from the top something made me grab the rail and push past its I was not sure but whatever it was I think it was a type of barrier. I go into the bathroom and well it was different a shelf over the bath with the water tank on it so you would need duck your head to have a bath. But we could manage. Going into the back bedroom the only room newly plastered but the burn marks on the ceiling were a bit odd. Tanith announced I am having this room I do not share my room with anyone especially not creepy ghost children. So, I donates that room to you. I walk into it was about 19ft long by 13ft wide 2 windows big old sash types an odd built-in cupboard in the alcove. It was freezing cold a boy stood there sheltering a smaller girl I said whom are you why are you here? Our father will not let us out we cannot go help us. I went downstairs felt the same barrier type thing. We signed up what is a few ghosts to us. We were to move in on the Saturday. So, I decided to go down scrub the place, light the fires and paint the first room. I planned to sleep there, had an airbed sleeping bag pillows, things for tea and music so thought I would do jobs late then fall asleep. I painted one bedroom and our kitchen, as it started go dark the atmosphere in the house changed it became very

Whispers of the Witch by NanyWytch

oppressive. I was not sure why then I saw a Victorian lady in a blue dress with an apron over walk past me towards the back-room I could hear the dress as it cascaded along the floor, her boots made a click sound from the metal segs underneath. As I followed her walking into the back room that moments before was decorated with old newspapers. I noticed the room had changed back to 1890, the range took place in the hearth with metal kettle hanging there. A pot was on the stove, a wooden table with a bench. 2 wooden chairs near the hearth. One of those pull-down clothes racks hung high over the top of the hearth with night dresses then the room switches back to how it was. Later on, I am in the front room that I has been painting, when I needs the loo I have shut all the doors let the back-room fire go out turned off the lights. As I come out the room to head up the stairs I see a rough looking man standing there in a collarless shirt. Big trousers held up with braces and a wide belt around them. He is tall and thick set with a mop of curly dark hair. But the feelings I am picking up is nasty. My stomach turns but I needs to pee. So, I goes up the stairs at the fourth step from top I grab the handrail run up the rest into the bathroom. As I come out I have that crawling feeling at the back of the neck, a cold shiver creeps down my spine. I step onto the top section of hall he is standing outside the back-bedroom staring at me with a gleam in his eyes. I start go down the stairs, when without warning at all I feel a hand on my back push me hard. Falling fast I grab the handrail to try steady myself spindles break with the speed of my fall. Several of them are now broken, my body is falling so fast I have to slow down or my head will hit those quarry tiles. Just as I see an old lady falling head smashing onto that same red quarry tile. Realising that its possibly how the last owner died. They said a fall. Then my foot catches on something it broken a piece 9f wood off the front of the stairs ripped open my ankle and back of foot. Once at the bottom I manage to sit, my leg is pouring with blood, it is around 3am I ring my friend who gets there in minutes. He packs the wound then picks me up fastens md onto the motorbike saying it will be faster this way. I had several stitches to my ankle and foot, but I was not going to allow some mean-spirited ghost stop me making a good home there. We released the children helping them leave Sarah appeared said thank you then left. We asked for him to leave but we were told he could not go yet, we asked why they said he has to see real love and acknowledge he was wrong to move on.

So, this angry minor stayed for several years, he frequently watched me in the bath or in bed he did not come downstairs at all simply stood up near the bathroom gradually the atmosphere went better it took time. We lived there incredibly happy for over 19 years it was a great home.

Whispers of the Witch by NanyWytch

Raped by a demigod.

I had this really odd dream where Richard was pushing me to go off with Vivian, but it felt very odd, he has never done anything like this before. My goddess said I should not go because there was something she could not see.

I woke up disturbed by the whole thing at breakfast I asked him about it. He said I had figure it out on my own. So off we went to the sorcerer's apprentice shop in Leeds, Saturday mornings were excellent. It had this coffee shop we could go to and anybody worth talking to would be there. I had some wonderful mornings there. This morning just the same come 1pm Viv had arrived suggested I go his house for the afternoon whilst Richard did something else it seemed very odd sort of pre- arranged somehow as Richard seemed be all for it. he said phone when you want picking up. So being rather naive at the time about different paths having different rules. I went with Viv I had only met him once before so did not really know him. He said his daughter would be there. We arrived it was this huge house in its own grounds, lovely gardens. We went inside it was fantastic old building, we sat in the music room to chat his daughter was doing university work on the dining room table. She brought us coffee and we began talking about all sorts of stuff. Then we talked about magic at no time did it seem odd, I fact it was relaxed and pleasant but maybe the wine helped and the sandwiches his daughter made. Back in the music room after the break for tea and cakes Viv was standing near the fireplace but at around dusk the atmosphere changed, had this oddness about it sort of hidden from view.

Viv was a small rounded potbellied man but this man near the hearth was not he was tall slender.muscular his hair was thick not balding. I felt odd I had this feeling now was time to leave so said I wanted call RBB collect me. I did not know where we were even. I knew it was miles from Dewsbury. So, I got up to walk to the phone at the end of the hallway which was quiet long, I got there dialled the number was waiting for the answer when I saw pan walking down the hall towards me, he was very tall, looked very dark and the power coming off him was very strong by time Richard answered I tried to say please come for me by this time pan was less than 3 ft. from me glaring right at me. The words that I said were not what I wanted at all. I said I am staying over will see you tomorrow. Richard asked if I was OK, I tried to say no but instead said yeah everything as it ought to be. A rather odd statement. Are you sure he said I really tried to say my words, but couldn't he be stopping me controlling the call?

After I put the phone down I said why did you do that? He replied because I can I arranged it I wanted your company this evening. We will eat drink wine it will be particularly good I can get to know you. I tried call on my goddess, but he said she cannot help you this is my domain you entered by your own free will.

I had no choice it seemed but to take part in this meal I had no idea what had happened as I left the music room or why Viv was not here. Viv was a kind and gentle man who had done well in his life. His daughter had left gone back to Leeds. So, we were alone. We ate a lovely meal he cooked drank some very lovely wine talked a lot about magic's at about 9pm

Whispers of the Witch by NanyWytch

I said I was tired wanted go to bed. He showed me upstairs he seemed to know the house well put me in a room where Viv's wife had slept said nightclothes were in the draw, why not take a nice relaxing bath light candles incense you will feel better. A god had never talked to me like this, before only my goddess. I took the bath lit candles incense then I locked the large bolt a Cross the door breathed a sigh of relief that I was now alone. I got into the bed fell asleep. Around 3am I was woken by the man coming into my room how he got through that solid locked door.

I struggled to open my eyes but saw pan on the bed removing the duvet. He laid over me I couldn't do anything to stop it I was stuck, I screamed out I struggled but then I couldn't move it was as if were frozen still he held me down, laughing he pulled open my legs, raped me this occurred more than once all I could do was watch it all happen. He got off me stood up as if nothing had just occurred of any consequence. I was crying wanting my goddess to help me I saw her at the window she said to me I tried to warn you, I cannot enter. He will not permit it. All I knew was it was not Vivian who had harmed me but pan. My goddess said I had to get up wash myself and I had to fight to get free of his will as he planned on keeping me there to spite her as the two of them hated each other by harming me it hurt her some kind of sick justice.

I went for a bath got dressed went downstairs, made a brew to calm, nerves then Viv came into the kitchen, I asked where he had gone last night. He replied Pan is my God he gave me something the terms were steep, he wanted to meet you spend time with your I had to agree I had no choice. I said take me back to Richard now. He said why what is wrong? I said nothing you can fix. I called Richard said we were coming early. When we got their I ran upstairs to the temple room, once Viv had gone Richard came up, he asked me what had happened why I had not come back. I told him then said pan raped me and Diana will hate me know she will not want me back not now.

Richard said he was woken at 3am by a very annoyed Diana she was shouting at him saying he should have protected me gone with me. He said she told him she could not help me because pan forbade her entrance into his domain. Richard said he now understood my dream, it was clear he was supposed help me make the choice. He did not.

Vivian found it hard to grasp that something untoward had occurred in his absence from his body. Gods have rules about each other's domain and servitors. None can enter without the consent of that god or goddess. Rhoda saw how upset and disturbed so had come to me to hug me talk to me crying I told her about the rapes and not being able stop it.

So, we did a cleansing ritual then Richard did a rite in Latin I saw Diana she held me tight I cried she said it was all ok now it was fixed.

I just felt so helpless that night I was not sure if it was because I has always been able see the Gods, they have always come to me. I had no idea why it was so only that it was. It made me quite different to even other witches if I mentioned it, they looked at me as if I were mad. Then I realised many had not seen one to speak to personally like I had. They feared them I could not understand why this was so. I had never felt fear of them not even when one was cross with me. It felt like it feels when your parents were upset with you. But that night knew only fear as he compelled me by force to say words not of my mind.

Vivian came back to the house to ask after me, Richard said I should tell him what had occurred. Vivian said pan had been his god for a long time, had done him favours helped him get along in business in his life. He made him amazingly comfortable indeed. That he had come to him saying he wanted to use his body for 24 hours to achieve something of his own. It was pan who chose the day and time for the exchange. Then it was pan who had met us outside of sorcerer's apprentice shop. Not Vivian

Viv was really upset to hear what had taken place at his home and indeed in his absence. Pan is a demi got not full god. Demi gods are half human half gods. There are many of them but they do not dwell amongst true gods as they are seen as being lower in status the stories of his music being haunting are true as it takes you into another realm like a dream world that is misty so you cannot fathom what or where you find yourself. Neither do you control your own actions.

Past meets present.

I was extremely excited today I was to get my new bed, the one we had made for us. I called my friend Allen up to come over, he lived just over the road. Allen was my very feminine guy University friend to me Allen was a girl not a boy. We were chatting as the men built my bed in my room. After Allen and I made it up ready to try, we fell onto it together. My husband Had arrived home into the back garden he had seen us in the room. Without any warning he was there, he stuck a spear at Allen's throat. Allen was against the wall; it was not my husband's voice. He came out with in a voice I had not heard since 1068 ad, why are you in my lady's bed chamber? This voice was my Norman cnicht from back then. Not my current husband yet they were one and the same person.

As he was holding Allen there a video memory played through my head it was back in 1068 in the castle as the base of the main stairs to the great hall. Where everything that was anything took place. There I saw as if it were right now Allen just as he was today in looks being held against a wall by a sword blade. With my cnicht saying When I tells you to fetch my sword boy I expect it to be in my hands promptly not when you get around to it, next time you keep me waiting I will not be so nice. The poor boy was quacking at the knees I had been coming down the stairs, when my lord said lady hold right there.

I was now in my room again trying to tell my lord that it was ok Allen would not harm me. But trying to get around this cnicht was almost impossible he was used to being obeyed. Back in 1068 he was one of the cnicht who had fought in 1066 at that battle where I lost my three brothers. As a result, I was married off to the man settling here who had been granted lands by the king. Being a high-born Saxon lady I was used to living to a high standard. I had a servant called Bryson. The event of my marriage was stranger than fact, as I was a healer but in 1068 a new Bishop had come to our land in Yorkshire. He began to systematically gain lands a title by accusing people 0f witchery and heresy. I had attended on a childbirth with Bryson we had needed turn the child he had then torn his mother at birth, we had tended her cleaned her, stitched her wounds and tended the child till they were ready be together. If we had not turned the child both parties would have died. Sometime later men came to my lands proclaiming I was using witchery, then took me away to the basement of some building I had sent Bryson to the castle to get the lord there. He had come with around a dozen men that was the first-time I had seen this lord. He was so handsome and the authority he held over people was impressive. The bishop protested at me being taken to the castle, to be heard. He claimed it was his duty as a soldier of God to cleanse the place of heathen ways. That using potions and herbs was indeed witchery. He said the family had told him of my meddling amongst good Christians on this land.

Whispers of the Witch by NanyWytch

I was but 16 years of age but in those days, it was late for a marriage, normally you were wed off as soon as you bled. Which was around 13 years old. My father had spoilt me my mother had taught me about the herbs and how to use them. Many a time I had sewn my father and brothers war wounds. At this time William was starting to Harrow the North, because some Saxons rebelled against the new system and laws that took land from Saxons to give away to his friends the very same day. After the lord had heard me talk about the woman, he dismissed the case. The bishop did not like this, but the Lord had taken a liking to me. His king had told him to seek out a woman of high-born status to marry. Once we had met it was arranged. He allowed me to keep practicing my healing, however my night-time visits to the wood to gather herbs were no longer alone. I was never permitted to leave unescorted as was my rank in life. We had a good marriage we loved each other deeply but some 7 years in he rode out to a battle and did not return.

I had fretted for him and not long after I had died. But here we were in this time together again, I tried to tell him poor Allen was scared he remembered too. I saw it on his face, he tried to speak but my lord said silence boy. I said please my lord it is only a boy; lady silence I will deal with you later allowing the servants here male servants indeed. Then just as sudden mark was back, now he said that just freaked me right out why was I trying kill Allen. I explained he said I saw pictures in my head a castle him me you, but our clothing was well Norman your dress was a lilac you had that girl with you the one from the village. Yes, I said you are remembering where you last saw Allen.

I watched the same sequence of pictures from my mind as you started to talk. Well I am so sorry Allen come let us have a drink. When we begin to recall our own past its normally because someone we have just seen or have come into contact with belongs in our soul family.

201 copyright Ashna Yates BSC 2020

Whispers of the Witch by NanyWytch

Healing

202 copyright Ashna Yates BSC 2020

Whispers of the Witch by NanyWytch

Things we learn when out with our parents were good things but as a child you forget. We would talk about plants that the gods gave us everything we needed something that is poison is next to the plant that heals.

When I was young I got a bad chest infection my gran said fetch her the brown wrapping paper and string. I did then she crushed camphor and cloves together added them to the grease from the goose blended it in her mortar. Then she pasted it onto the brown paper I watched wondering how this was going heal me

Then she cut it like a vest tied it onto my chest and back then made me a medicine from colts' foot, honey, pine, liquorice root. I fell asleep in the morning my chest was better. I guess today it would be like applying Vick, giving them Calpol.

I loved the old ways but when the BMA came to our herbal shop took away our cough syrup, they came back saying we had to remove the coltsfoot. We explained it was the active ingredients that with the others lifted the mucus from the chest. Well, we do not want the pharmaceutical companies all complaining as this works there is does not. But then it will not do anything except heal a sore throat which will bring it in line with the others.

Gran taught me stuff like this for an open wound get oak moss cover the wound after cleaning it to stench the blood. Then cover and leave after a few hours stitch up the wound apply the moss again or make a bread poultice.

Whispers of the Witch by NanyWytch

We grew herbs but the best part was the making things, but then you grow up go playing out and forget thus stuff. Lucky for me though the other witches know as well so if you forget like I did today I said to my sister witch that's fennel, mint, chamomile, lavender and she said lady's mantle It is a great thing having herbal books now however mine is very old copy of Culpeper's herbal the content is mostly in old English, but the pictures are so lovely.

Today not many people would know that feverfew is good for migraines bruise a leaf make a tea its bitter unless you add honey. When we did an interview for a magazine, they were with us the whole day but the piece they wrote was great it was for a teenage magazine a bit like Jackie.

Tanith did her interview at 15 years old then I did mine, the pictures are OK I was not really pleased with mine, but the article was the important part Over time I have been in the papers, on radio, and TV talking about the craft. One day we were invited to channel 4 to do a live broadcast it was Beltane. We were to do a love spell live on air at 11pm. We were on after the new band. However, the priest with me had never done TV work but said he was OK. So, it came to our bit I set up whilst talking about what we were going to do he was supposed to speak the spell. He stood there silent he had frozen seeing the sheer numbers in the studio. I took over it cutting the view of him out did the spell then answered questions

I do not like love spells and I will not do them, because someone can get hurt by it. For example, the last time I was asked for one was a woman whom came with a photo of a man saying this is her man he had run off with another woman whom she had a photo off she wanted me to break them up help her get him back. When I checked out the names the two were married to each other she was the other woman he had dumped to stay with his wife.

So, I refused. I have not agreed do once since.

LODGE STREET

Whispers of the Witch by NanyWytch

We were to move to Haworth for my health I had this urge to go home. We had thought Marks work transfer would take the 6 weeks, hence allowing us time find a house there. How it worked out was his transfer was through in one week, we had one day to go see properties. I took this small cottage because it was part way up main street, which happened to be the street the first masons Lodge was on, hence lodge street. The day we were moving I opted go there first so as boxes arrived I could start to unpack them. Plus, my snakes needed travel with me all three of them.

Two Albinos with red eyes plus my orange corn snake. Now they are 7ft long and heavy, I loves them like children my fondness for snakes began in ancient Egypt when I lived in the temple I had been given to Isis at age 5 to become a priestess. My life before thus was in Babylon where my goddess was Ishtar. I began to place books on a shelf at the base of the wooden stairs. When I turned my back get more books, the shelf fell over. Puzzled I checked the floor for uneven places checked the wall then put them back my plan was to ask Allen to fasten it to the wall secure it. It fell again I knelt on the floor picking up books saw a man standing on 3rd step up an old man dressed in clothes of the 1800s, I said did you do this? Well, tis my house he said my chair sits right here near the hearth see. I said its now my house and guess what there is no hearth or fire mores the pity it would have been nice have a fire. She did it that woman, she ripped out the stone stairs that curled around the hearth where cellar door was. Then put this contraption in called em stairs. I hate it. Tis my house I was born here I died here too. She stole the cellar blocked off the door put it for her daughter's house next door. We had a butcher shop here lived in the other half not here this was just two rooms. My father, mother and 4 lads slept up there. Then when they died I had it as eldest lad, married my wife had two children we all slept up there. 2 big beds set of draws that was it down here we had rockers chairs bench table and a loom.

But the midden was straight across from here, and those toilets flooded and leaked shit and piss down the hill. Stench and flies in summer because butchers threw the waste in the midden.

Open sewer ran down main street in them days my children and wife got cholera lots of folk got it half the graveyard full of em babies died incredibly young, my wife lost 3 young ones under 2 before our lads lived.

You go up there read them stones, we have a grave in top corner near the wall. Then why are you here? Tis me house why should I leave tis mine see. I see but I could help you go to your wife and boys. Now tis freedom from her nagging I wants. Tis alright thus way I gets find out stuff.

I agreed move the bookcase for his chair, the rocker.

Problem was the kettle would turn itself on boil then he would brew up for himself not me. But when I was cooking, he would come behind me and say what is the making lass, I would say sausage and potatoes beans, for dinner. Thaws can eat meat in week on Tuesdays. Yeah, then thaws must be right rich. We only had meat on special days maybe twice a year. We had bread and cheese, or pottage mostly or a stew I might catch a rabbit for pot but twas nearest we got to meat. Lest I got scrap end of lamb cheap. We were poor see, mill wages were only 6d a day for 12 hours hard graft oh yea they gave you pottage at morning break and stew at afternoon break hunk of bread or them children would have died from workhouse 10 mills in our village. Could leave a job get another in afternoon.

But the new folk in them houses at bottom near railway they were Irish farmers they came when bottom fell out of land. But we up here in original village had nought do with em stuck up an all that. When I baked, he would come sniffing about oh I nor had cake lass could I have a bit, yeah but how do you plan on eating it. Well I thought I might be allowed step into you a bit so as I can taste it no way I said I dun no allow it. But thaws a witch are not thee lets the gods come into thee. That is vastly different.

Good parts where he would lurk about on stairs pull folks hair, he also set off smoke alarms at night on purpose because he claimed be lonely. Or he would say she is on way here for rent. Yeah, will give it her later. Go away. He was a harmless old man simply did not want move on some people do not they just stay home carry on living there. They see only what they wish to see. When we were leaving I said once we are gone set them alarms off every day as she will come in paint over the damp rent it out again you make sure they don't stay it's not right her getting rent money and not fixing it. Do not worry he said I do not like her so will do it more a once a night new folks will not even stay 3 months. I said do you want to go to your family I can help you. It seems a shame you are staying here

I thank you but I will stay.

I was sad to leave him there in 5 years I had become fond of him.

Whispers of the Witch by NanyWytch

.

Darker times

Whispers of the Witch by NanyWytch

During my life I have been lucky as the gods have stayed close by me which has given me insight I do not think I would not have had otherwise. When I lived in Manchester in a flat shared with other witches, we had John who was a pure-bred Celt he had beautiful long red hair and a nice red beard he was into Celtic magic's. Adrian was into Thelma and high magic's. Allen well let us just say he was a drinker but had come from a darker path. I had met him when he owned a shop in Manchester, he read tarot cards at psychic fayres like I did. Its where I met a lot of people that I knows all into their own paths. One sab bat we decided spend it together do a ritual celebration, so I transformed the empty room with the help of William our x army friend and 2 of his mates we painted walls we found an altar we set it all up ready for that night. We had sent Allen out in the morning for cake, bread, wine we had given him over £50 to purchase the bagels wine at the Jewish market where we always bought bread and bagels. By. Mid-afternoon he had not returned with the things. So, Adrian went to find him. When they came back Allen was bladdered with drink he had not bought one item instead he had drunk the money. Adrian dropped him onto his bed. We were doing some readings in the other room and practicing what we wanted achieve that night. When people from different path merge it can be remarkably interesting especially when you say they can call a gate their way. I enjoyed learning how others did things. As we were all sitting in the lounge, I heard a crash we went to investigate, Allen was in the newly made temple smashing it up he upturned the altar and my very old goddess figures hit the floor along with the only photo I had of my children. I went into the room from the door grabbed him around the neck I had his own knife at his throat and was screaming about desecration of sacred space wanting old lore. I cut his neck a bit not much with his own knife. William and the two army lads were trying get me off him amongst the debris that had been our sacred space I was screaming about what he had done that the goddess demanded his blood. When William got me off him got the knife, he held me tight I screamed this horrible gluteal sound that came from the bowels of the earth. William said he had seen this before someone connected to the gods like I am has such a close relationship with them that they pick up their feelings and want their revenge for desecration of sacred space. It came from the destruction of temples in the east.

I sat amongst the broken things picked up my old bast goddess who now had no ears, my Aphrodite who now had no head. The picture of my children broken and torn. Why would he do this when he was a witch too, what could have been in his head. It was not just the drink as this was pure anger at something. He fell onto his bed crying that I had nearly cut his throat. I had nicked it about half an inch just far enough away from his jugular vein but enough to let his blood run. He must have gone to sleep. We rebuilt the room reconnected it, John had just got to the market in time buy the things we needed to put with the meats we had cooked the vegetarian nut roast and quiche as two members were vegetarian and one was a non-drinker so fruit juice for him not ale or wine. Everything ready we all robed up and we began the rite that night was going to be quite different as William was going to be the high priest for us. When we swopped leaders about the rites were always different. Yet we all learnt from it another way to do the same thing. We had concluded the rites were just having fun and eating food. When we heard a disturbance from the room where we had left Allen sleeping it off. Thinking it would be him William myself and Adrian come out of the room. When we enter the room, a person was inside Allen's body it was not Allen. The person addressed William saying where is this place merlin, like he knew him from somewhere, then he said why is this body sickly and dirty I need to wash. Fetch water to me, we took him to the bathroom turned on the taps he jumped backwards. Arggghh tis witches magic how can I wash in this bowl. We said it was witches who lived here, and it was magic called plumbing the water can climb walls. No, he said water flows down not up. Tis magic that is all. He said fetch me herbal medicine to heal this body. I made some brought it to him now in clean clothing well a white robe. He put his finger in the cup said awe I know this it will not harm me it has colt of foot in here I smell it with vervain as well as lavender are you trying put me to sleep? Igraine why are you here? Who else is here we took him into our scared room sat him down offered him wine and food he accepted some bread cheese and chicken? He sat and ate food with us then said he felt weary needed to lay down. Do we take him back to the cleaned bed laid him down he said thank you for a nice dream? Then he slept it would be the herbal drink I made. We had a good night. Allen came in at some point joined us not sure when but around about 11.30pm he got rather strange saying they will kill me they will kill me I need make a phone call. He dressed I dressed quickly in skirt top shoes followed him why I had no idea, but I was told follow him you need to know this. He was in the phone box saying he could not make it; it had all gone wrong she is a crazy bitch almost slit my throat. A man's voice on the phone said you're an idiot we told you to get rid of her for good we said you were close enough to kill her it was what you agreed to do because we helped you out of the shit when you drank the money away given you to bring the business back on track, we pulled you out put you back at the top of your game now you owe us you stupid fool, you are drunk. What about the new ones, yes there were some great people there all possible no you get your arse here for midnight we have business to conclude and dress properly this time I cannot she followed me no matter just do it. I grabbed Allen he said it is not my fault they wanted me to destroy you they said I had to harm you. I said who are they he said they worship Hecate are left hand path people. I have to dress and go. Where to! The meeting they will kill me I failed again he was really frightened. But we got dressed he wore a white shirt black trousers I wore a long black skirt white top my protection jewellery then I followed him he knew I was following him, but he did not care. He led me to a club in Manchester as I was walking up the steep steps following Allen. A voice said we are with you it is dangerous now listen as you walk in there will be three behind you two flanking your left two on your right two more in front of you. Go straight to the toilets brush your hair add your lippy and then get your warrior face on. If we are doing this go straight to where Allen is grabbing his arm say come on mate I will buy you a drink do not give him the choice just take him to the bar and look around you as you walk there. The ones in charge are the three at the table. Be careful we do not yet know what they plan to do. So, we are going take the lead. Once you have your drink down it in one then walk over to the table plant your hands on it. Say to the one in the middle. That it is nice to put a face to the voice on the phone saying you wanted me dead. Well I am so sorry, but you see Allen belongs to me now, I let his blood earlier so have my links now. I do believe you want me dead so sorry to disappoint but the Gods have a message for you. Broken oaths no longer hold water. Anyway, it is time for me to leave I would not want stop your rites to Hecate.

I admit that night scared me big time knowing some other people wanted me dead. I had no idea why or if I had ever come across them before.

Witch Dr

Richard asked me go visit his friend in prison, I asked why he said he wanted me learn about the darker sides to magic. That Owen was a good African voodoo man. I had no idea what to expect having never been into a prison before. I did not like all the clanging of doors as they were locked behind you. I had taken a bag of things for him he had asked for on the phone. Plastacine, a red match box car, pens, paper, fags match. Once sat down we started talking a guard came over said you should not visit him he is a waste of space and he does not deserve you. Asking Owen what that was about he said that guard hated him, spat in his food or knocked it onto the floor.

We sat there playing with the Plastacine we made people and a wall that guard kept coming over making nasty comments till I said do you mind I only have 30 minutes left so back off.

We sat a man inside the car, and we ran it into the wall many times we both did it. Then he drew a Sigel said some words and lit the paper saying take it now. Then he stamped on it picked up the ashes placed them inside the car. We talked more he said he will not bother us anymore. By time my next visit came I heard the guard crashed his car that night into the wall near the gate. He was killed instantly as he was not wearing his seat belt.

I said to Owen did we do that maybe he said who is to say or not how magic works. He was getting out in a few days I agreed come see him once he was settled.

The next time I saw him he was dressed very smartly we went out to dinner, then to a club, we sat at the bar the place was a bit strange as you had been a member to come in. The dance floor was in the middle I loved dancing, but Owen came to me said not here later. Ok I said not understanding why. Later he told me why. Another time I went out the pub with him, sat down at a table with a drink in corner as Owen said he had a bit of business to attend to said he wouldn't be far away, but he had paid for several brandy's and Baby sham for me.

A bloke came sit near me with a shoulder bag, he said can you roll a spliff! I said yes but I does not put a lot of tobacco in mine as I do not smoke. He said OK hands me the large fag papers and stuff I break quiet a lot into the spliff. We light it and are smoking it getting really chilled out. It was half gone when he asked me who was buying my drinks. I said I am with Owen over there, the man panicked took the spliff off me put it out. He said Jesus Christ girl he will kill me if he sees you smoking his weed. It is his weed I say so we are ok. No, we are not I have not paid him for it yet, I was so chilled out I said awe come on give it back its only one spliff not a bag full. No, I cannot at that moment Owen came over said to Joe I do believe you owe me money £500 have you got it? Are you OK girl, I said do not be mean you him he is nice? Your stoned he said he grabbed Joe said have you given her drugs. I said Owen listen I rolled the joint I smoked it. So, it is me you can shout at. No, my lady it is not he is a drug dealer he pushes it onto anyone he can he does not give a crap. But I was having fun you were ignoring me. I am sorry but he still has not paid me. Joe hands over money Owen slaps him on the back says see Harry at the bar. Joe gets up to leave. OWEN sat near me saying you smoked nearly a whole joint. Yeah, I said its good shit laughing I was as high as a kite.

Come on let us get you back to the house, I was pretty drunk as well as stoned. OWEN put me to bed I slept it off woke up I had on silk pyjamas I walked into the lounge it was full of people I sat on the sofa Owen handed me jerk chicken and rice said eat it you haven't eaten all day. I loved his chicken and rice with peas I loved the African bread he made too. He was an excellent cook. We went out that night

Whispers of the Witch by NanyWytch

where I did dance till 3am it was an ace night. The next morning an African man was knocking on the door at 10am we were sleeping having been out. I answered the door he said I need the witch Drs all I need him now. I said he was sleeping he said his daughter went to a party but did not come home so he went there found her as a zombie. Now it is not what is on the films dead people eating others nothing like that Africa has many old ways, they can turn a person into an emotionless being by removing their essence into a bottle or jar what is left is an empty vessel. It cannot function like we do it can only take one instruction at a time like walk forward 4 steps, turn right, walk forward 5 steps. Turnabout, stop. Owen told the man he would help but it would be £300 fee, the man agreed. Owen said I need your help for this the girl has been messing with Dambulla. This is the result of that. He said I needed stay with the family, take the money. Make a drink keep them away from his room. I agreed he then said whatever is in her he would send through the wall into me as it could not harm me. Then after the work is done, he will get it from me. I sat on the chair we placed next to the wall dividing us. At some point in the next two hours, it came into me. The girl was now back to being a normal African teenager. Her father slapped her hard-said messing about was new banned in his house. The girl hugged Owen saying I did not know I did not know thank you for my life. Once they had left Owen said in my room is a plate on it is bread salt and wine you must eat it then lay down place this talisman on your stomach I will come. I feel asleep vague memories of him drawing on my stomach and legs, arms, when I woke it had gone. We had a great day, but people kept asking for things from him. The rite he had done tired him and me. The very next day at an early time heard people in the house. When I came out the room, people were bringing in flowers, wine, food filling up the kitchen with these things the floor was covered in these trays of food. Yet they were bringing more the whole kitchen was full to the brim in offerings to the gods and for Owen. The father said you are a white mamma you helped my child. Hands me an envelope with cash, I say I cannot, yes you can my baby is safe now. You both brought her back to me I knows about this take it. When Owen woke up, he said well it worked was hard to do but it worked. Yes, he said it us a custom of my land if the witch doctor helps you, your family thanks him anyway they can. Usually, they cook food for him bring the gods flowers and other thing food is one of them my altar has gifts on it for them. It is how it works. Yes, I calls on darker gods than you and my path is different but light and dark mix well together they are the twilight the between times. You are special because the gods honour you with a closeness many would desire. Yet it cannot be taken as the gods choose whom they talk to.

I just love goat patties I just could not get enough of them and jerk chicken oh it is a wonderful dish. My life has been varied so much this is the only life I have had so far where I was not killed because I was a witch. I never had love or children or a man who cares for me in such a profound way before. So, if my writing can help one other learn about the crossing over to other realms it has been a good journey.

Angels

Whispers of the Witch by NanyWytch

As my teacher of some 33 years lay dying, he wanted me, he had sat up in a chair in his lounge. As I arrived I saw an angel standing at the door around 7ft tall dressed in this metal that glimmers his boots were shiny too, his hair was brown he if human might have been 35, he smiled at me as I walked into the room. Richard said come I hugged him for the last time. I tried not to be sad that day as I did not want him to see me cry as in our world dying is not a sad thing it is a good thing, its release from our lives here on earth. We ourselves do not die we move on. Two more angels were in that room both of them tall like the one near the door the one near the window was bright with red clothing a metal breast plate sandals knew the name of only one of them. He had his hands-on Richards shoulders putting energy into him so he could do this one last thing. He told the other angels this is whom he has waited for look at the pure love between them no other bond is needed between student and teacher. I sat in the chair an angel standing behind me. I felt so honoured to see them like this. Richard said if you looked at my books from where you are is there one you would like to have? The angel behind me leant in whispered pick the big red book. I said yes, the big red one, Richard said to get it. This was a first print of the golden dawn rites and teachings it had been signed by the author and given to Richard as a gift now Richard signed it to me giving me this special gift. Saying you will not need any other book for high magic's now.

When I am gone from this body I will always be available to you as I will not reincarnate this time but become one of the guides of souls instead.

Now you know the library of Alexandria that is where we will meet so we can continue your learning. I hugged him again and then I left to talk you his wife as the angels said he was very tired now he had completed his very last task. He died that night with his lady holding him.

I miss him so much he was more than a teacher to me. We have a song we used to sing that each time I hears it I cry a lot.

I have not cried at deaths of people for an exceptionally long time because I know they are not dead just moving onto another realm on a different vibration than ours.

GEORGE FIRSOFF

Whispers of the Witch by NanyWytch

I had known George an exceptionally long time when he decided to move to near me in Stoke-on-Trent Staffordshire. We would go out to lunch; George was rather eccentric in many ways. He spoke with an Oxford dialect, yet often he dressed like a tramp. Sometimes he came in his pyjama top instead of a shirt. But George was just lovely.

He spent a lot of hours talking with me, about magic's. About stone henge, he did a lot of work regarding stone henge.

George was present at my hand fast back in 1994, he gave us a glass chalice.

When George confided in me about his bowel cancer, he said he did not want the surgery. He also said he was averse to putting chemicals in his body.

Many pagans do not want unknown chemicals in their bodies some of my Vikings are the same.

George bought a house 10-minute walk to mine, across a lovely park. We would walk there amongst the trees, sit on the grass, even lay down watching the clouds drift by. Our days were very quietly spent.

I knew he was in a lot of pain so visited him each day, made up his bed set out his room to make him comfortable. But George laid on top of all this clean bedding on a dirty bedroll. I talked to him about infections as he was now fitted with a bag for his bowel and bladder.

He opted for medication to stem the spread but refused chemotherapy. He did have a few lots of radiotherapy though. But his cancer had got to stage four. He told me he was dying, and he wanted me let his friends know, whom he worked with on the stone henge project.

However, George caught an infection was admitted to hospital, he gave them my number asking me come. Of course, I went many times over those last weeks. Collecting things for him.

I even put cream on his feet as the nurses were not allowed because of infection. I brushed his hair washed his pyjamas took more. Which because he hoarded books, took forever to find.

Georges house was like a maze of towers of great books. One room full of his parent's things. He told me to take the photos and important papers to mine. Which of course I did.

Then on a visit not long before Yule, George became quite ill again he was on morphine so slept a lot. But he was wide awake on this visit he even seemed a bit better. He was incredibly happy he asked me get him some socks. As he said he was coming to my house for Yule. I agreed he needed new socks and new shirt for that.

Speaking to the nurse she said he is not going home; he is dying, and he knows he is. Often, she said patients dying become quite happy, excited about going home. She suspected they did not mean to a house.

George died a few hours later, we did a pagan rite for him, at our house. As he had no family who wanted see him, we arranged the funeral. It was considerably basic as we did not have time find addresses phone numbers, we had wait 6 weeks to be able carry out his final wishes. Which were to have his ashes planted under an Ash tree in the park we spent time in. He said it had to be planted between our houses near the way we walked.

I had found 6 of his friends to invite, who all made it, we went to the park with his ashes, the council had selected the spot, dug the hole for us. They stayed for our pagan remembrance of such a good friend.

We had each brought photos of George with us and a gift to help him on his journey. We talked about how we had met him how many years we had known him. We spoke about our days together funny things between us. Then we placed our gift on top of the ashes.

I had his socks to keep his feet warm, half bottle of whiskey was fed the earth. Red wine and cakes were shared. The photos placed in with him. So, he was not lonely, after we had all given our gifts to the earth or placed into the hole it was filled in. We planted daffodil bulbs there around that tree.

Then we went to mine for food and wine, the council people said it was the nicest funeral they had known as none of us were melancholy. We explained about how we see death.

Finally, we went to the house to tidy it up pack things up. His mates asked for some books. Which would only end up in a skip if not taken. So, we permitted them take some.

Some weeks later we had to empty the house so gave away to charity all his furniture which was nearly new. Then we had taken his car to the scrap man, his house was sold but the mortgage company were owed money by then so not much was left. We gave this to the cancer charity and hospice where he spent his last days.

Whispers of the Witch by NanyWytch

The Old woman

Whispers of the Witch by NanyWytch

In the complex of flats in which we resided in Macclesfield the row just below us led to the play group and other places. Around the fourth flat along this block was a ground floor flat in which resided an old woman. She was always shouting at the children walking past her flat. She would chase them onto the grass with her broom saying get off my garden when they were not on her lawn. All the children started to call her the mad woman who was always cleaning her windows. Nobody knew why she hated children so much but to her they were more like rats.

One day she was cleaning her windows again up a ladder, she misjudged a step and fell breaking her hip and arms. She was taken to hospital. Weeks pass she is not back we ask about her they said she had died in the hospital. Sometimes spirits who die at hospital just go home as they do not know they are dead, so they try to carry on with the life they had before they died. Obviously by now the flat had been rented out to a young couple it having two bedrooms. A few months after they moved in the woman asked me to come round the flat. She wanted to book a tarot party for her mother and some friends. We were talking over coffee when a tall handsome looking male came into the kitchen, He saw me saw the tarot deck we had been talking about. He lost it he grabbed my arm said get out of here I am having no witches inside my home go on leave he pushed me outside the door. The poor woman Wendy was so angry with him she had tried to talk to her husband about something being wrong with the flat.

I guess it was week later at around 9pm at night, the knocking on the door was loud I did not want the children woken up so went down to answer it. The man who had thrown me out of his flat was standing on my doorstep. He said to me You have to help me; the flat has something there it trapped my children in the room with it. I cannot get into them it will not allow it.

I stood there not feeling anything at all, I said first and foremost I do not have to help you. Secondly an apology would be nice to start. Thirdly I could ask for compensation for the lost earnings you deprived me of £100 from the tarot party Wendy was arranging with me at her mother's place.

Anything but please help me I am begging you I do not know what to do I am scared it will hurt them please help me I am so sorry for not being understanding about what my wife was doing that day. I did not know I thought she was dreaming it all up. I am a logical man but talk of spirits and demons I just do not believe in them.

I asked him inside to try understand what was going on in the flat, he said a few weeks ago they came back from work and the furniture was all different. Some old woman was sitting inside their lounge. She said it was her house and we had to leave here. We tried to explain to her that she had died at the hospital and the flat was ours now. She threw things at us our ornaments were all broken by her. She was terribly upset. We went stay at Wendy's parents place a few days hoping it would calm down if we were not there.

However, when we came back all our things were scattered about it was like someone had been in there and pulled everything from the draws thrown them into the hall. The old woman was stood there yelling get out this is my house. It got so bad we took the girls away for another couple of weeks we would go back during the day tidy up the mess. Sit and talk trying to decide how to solve this issue. I needed go to work, so did Wendy the girls needed go to school so we really had to move back in.

That was today we moved back in cleaned the place but as soon as it was dark there, she was ranting and raving at us. We had put the girls to bed in the small bedroom in bunks we had set up that day. We had all new furniture in that room including carpets. The woman went into that room she slammed the door shut saying she would make us leave. She was yelling at the girls we could hear her, but we could not get into the room at all. We looked through the window at the girls they were both on the top bunk together huddled in a corner. They looked terrified. So, I came here. Wendy said you would be able help us. I do not

understand how a dead person can have so much rage and power.

I said I will help I need gather some things, but I do need your help and Wendy's, you see a family light is bright if you stand together have you been arguing recently yes why? Because spirits try to cause discord as they feed on that energy, if a person has died suddenly and doesn't actually know they are dead, first they go home try to live the life they had, they try to talk to people, they try shopping for food obviously they cannot. People walk right through them cannot see or hear them. So, they then get angry, the more they cannot face the fact they are now dead the angrier they become. Often, they simply stay in the house do not do anything except watch. But sometimes if they were nasty people in life, they are even nastier when dead.

As we walked to his flat, I told him how he and his wife needed help me by being together in this and providing the girls with love and talking to them I said the light of you two will get us into the room. As soon as I get the door open you are to take the girls and leave me in there alone to talk to her.

A lot of noise was going on in It side the room it sounded as if things were being smashed to pieces. It took some time to persuade it to open the door I used getting the children out of her room. Apparently, this room was her bedroom.

Once we gained admission Geoff did as I asked, he lifted both girls down took them away to hug them and reassure them it was going to be ok. I went into the room; the place was smashed up. I said to her we needed to talk about what she Is doing. She turned on me shouting at me that she knew whom I was that I was a witch and had to stay away from her as she believed in god. I said I need you to show me what you see in this flat that angers you so much. She said they stole all my things they stole it is what they did my sisters brooch has gone and the pictures too. They must have them I need it back. I said to her then help me to find where they are for you. She said they are in the place they were before, but I cannot get them. It does not let me get them. Awe I said you cannot pick them up. No, I cannot I do not know why I can break things throw things but not pick up the things very precious to me. I asked where they were? Under there she said pointing to the floor. So, I got a screwdriver from Geoff and we opened the floorboards up a tin box was slid into the space. Pulling it out I sat on the chair with the woman next to me she was calm now. We opened it and inside was photos a brooch and money. I told her that she could not take these things with her when she goes into the light. She said she had worked that out herself, that some bright light keeps showing up, but she was afraid go there as she needed know where her things were. I asked about relatives she had none. I asked what she felt we ought to do with the pictures she said to burn them please. Then I asked if she would allow me pin the brooch to her dress. She said yes so that is what we did. My next task was about the money around £200 in notes. She said it was for my holiday maybe that family ought to have it because I did mess up the place a lot as I was so angry about being dead and not getting my stuff.

I agreed that it would be a nice gesture and that she ought to be the one tell them, she said she didn't like children, asking her why she said hers had died of the fever in the 1930s. she lost all her family to scarlet fever. When she saw children, it reminded her of her loss. She had been alone ever since she was 94 years young when she died.

We opened the door I asked the couple to come into the room so they could see her, she said to them I am sorry for what I did it was my anger at the loss of the only pictures of my own children. I am giving you the money and do whatever you want with it now I must go I am ready.

I called on the guardian angels they came she went with them into the light she was now free.

The flat became peaceful and a wonderful home for the family Geoff gave me half the money and we blessed the house that night with a party of sorts all was well with their world once more.

Physical medium

Whispers of the Witch by NanyWytch

I mentioned before that my youngest brother was a physical & mental medium, in 1968 when he was born, he was very unwell. He had caught a virus at the hospital the drs said to my mother after 2 months that he would die because he had lost so much of his birth weight. Mother was distraught without telling my father she went to a spiritual healer. So, toots as I called him got better, initially mother would not care for him so I did she only take an interest after he was 3 years old till then I had been his mother.

Once he had grown up, he went off to college like most young do with his best friend Karl in Preston. Some months later I started to hear him calling my name on the astral saying he needed me to find him. I dismissed this at first, but it became louder, so one day I said to Mike we are going to Preston find my brother he moved mum has wrong address for him. We drove to Preston we sat near the train station for coffee the children all had juice and crisps. Following the voice I could hear I guided mike to the street it was coming from. Finding the house was going to be harder as there were so many on both sides of the street. So, I told the children we were going play a game called find uncle Terry I said you all know his voice try listen see if you can find him after a few minutes of walking up the road Tanith yelled out he's in here upstairs shall we go see. We tried the door it was open, so we expected someone be inside, we walked around it was most certainly a student house needed a good clean. We went upstairs one-bedroom door was open it was my brother he was laid in the bed with a fever, he was all dirty and it looked like he had been laid there more than a day. Trouble was his legs and feet were covered in mud. Dried on mud. Mike made coffee we cleaned him up dressed him said we were going pack his things. He said go next door into Karl's room he has my magic books and journals, I asked why he replied I was losing days then weeks so Karl said he would record it all for me. We collected everything belonging my brother from the room, Karl had more than terry ever knew.

We drove home to Macclesfield to take care of him, he slept a lot initially, but I noticed some rather odd occurrences, he would leave the room mid conversation say he needed the loo. What came back was often not my brother. On some occasions it was just a spirit who was lost. Other times something more sinister happened something had come home with my brother, was residing inside him. He took himself off for walks. My brother did not do walks not long ones he preferred be sat on the computer.

Terrys version.

Once we were in college it was great for a while, we went to a party with some friend's part way through the night they decided do Ouija board, they were laughing joking swearing most of them very drunk but when the glass flew off the table the girls were at, they all scattered leaving me sat there. It came home with me, then the next day we were invited to go a ritual in the woods we thought ace never done this before might be fun. We went to some caves and these people all in black did this ritual I do not know if I was drugged or not, but everything felt like a dream and not real. They killed something I do not know what my mind was all-over the place things were dancing about me and the noise in my head made the music louder till it was just buzzing like a thousand bees inside my head. After this back-home I would go to class in the morning but later wake up here all dirty not recall where I had been. Days went missing that I have no idea where I was or what I did nothing. Then a week then two, I kept seeing this dessert or these moors where it was it was a desolate place. Then Karl would wake me asking if I was going eat. I do not know how long this had been going on before I got sick. So, I called my sister over the astral knowing she could help me I did not feel right I knew it was there all the time.

My girls were excited that uncle tes was coming stay because he could enthral a whole room of children with his super Cindy stories and professor gotalotofgobber. So, they were expecting him tell them stories, but he was too ill to do so. At odd times he was ok, and we did some mediumship work I needed see how he controlled things as I had a suspicion that this was the root cause of it. For direct voice, a spirit only overshadowed you it did not enter your body. But the physical medium side spirits walked through him into our reality. One such spirit was called Talagmar he described himself as a warrior of time, he said he would help against the spirit called Peter who wanted harm the old wise woman from 1645AD.

We asked him what year he had lived he replied 1312AD. How do you know the witch? We met near the canal a few days ago I was lost. Say hello to Peter for me will you,

Talagmar she suspected was peter, general peter Mathew's died in the battle for the key to life. In 1645Ad but unlike other spirits he did not move on he stayed angry and hateful as he was in life. He has followed me through time over and over again wanting to harm me again it was not enough to have me killed that day not for him. It was not enough that they burnt down my cottage he had ran in when I said the key was behind the hearth, but the roof fell in, he died screaming curses after me.

Talagmar was very convincing that he was not Peter he arranged meet me in otherworld form to talk. He said come to Tegs nose to the old pagan altar there at midnight.

Whispers of the Witch by NanyWytch

We were going to go out of body in astral form my warrior was coming with me he armed himself as if he were going to battle all I had was my athame. We went from the temple room that night Teg was a giant who had fallen onto the hill up near the old quarry. There was a 100 foot drop off one side at this place into that old quarry. The other side was paths and hills at the top was the stone altar made from his elbow. Pagans met up there it was quiet at night when the moon was up, it lit the sky like a hundred-watt bulb. We arrived first so we took the high point, we knew more than one was coming we could see them coming up the hill. Talagmar my brother and someone else whom spirit called Toby said he fed my brother decease and lies who tried hold back as my brother joined us. We hugged then he stood back neat Talagmar. Suddenly without any warning the other person came running towards us armed with a sword. My warrior said stand away, it was urgent I did not know which way to step I chose wrong as he drew his blade I was cut across the shoulder just above my heart. I fell to the floor losing blood quickly. I saw my warrior fight it was over quickly then he was by my side again he scooped me up in his arms called his horse to him with a whistle his black beautiful steed came up the hill we road that night like the darkness rides the sky. We were then in 512ad at my castle he carried me to my room into my bed laid me down sent for the healer, he then stood guard at the door facing outwards expecting something. A woman in a white nightdress was crying near the window they say it was my mother. There were men outside the room arguing about what to do about their lady injured the wizard was not here they had sent for the village healer instead. Talagmar arrived wanting to see me but my warrior saw him off saying it was all his fault I lay injured now.

The woman Bryson from the village came to me she stank she was dirty even her hands were grubby. I said take her away clean her do not let her touch me. She ignored me began making poultice from oak moss bread and valerian root. She mashed it all down into a green mush spread it onto linen applied it and strapped me up. She gave me lavender and chamomile tea to help me sleep saying I needed rest.

When I awoke in my body I couldn't use my left arm had this red mark just where I had been cut it took weeks to heal it has been said that if you die outside your body at any time you will die here at the same time as the link is cut.

My brother still had something inside him it was starting take over his whole persona changed his attitudes his voice his feelings everything was changing we had no idea how long it had been there. We decided do an exorcism using high magic's and a triangle of art for containment. Inside our circle this time. We set things up waited till it was my brother in the body then walked him in knowing this demon could not walk out as easy as my brother had stepped into it. We invoked the archangels to assist us in expelling this thing. At one stage it saw my Tanith he called to her in my brother's voice asking her take him out of here. We told her it was not her uncle to leave the room she was a good child. It took several hours to free my brother but once freed we closed him down sealing him so nothing could get back through. Even today years after he is still afraid open himself to spirit.

My girls enjoyed having their uncle home he did tell them stories in fact it was a birthday party whilst he was with us he had 20 children sat on the floor so quiet you would have thought the place empty when parents arrived we said shhhhhhhhh listen they asked for the magic spell to mesmerise children this way we pointed at my brother he was the story teller of our coven

1068

Whispers of the Witch by NanyWytch

The past

One cannot change the past only learn from it; this story is about the year 1068

The Normans were now in charge of our Saxon homeland, A Norman lord had been given the castle on the hill. He altered it making it bigger adding more rooms to the upper floor all that remained of the original was now pretty much gone apart from the great hall and fireplace.

Memories are rather strange things just like the past, I knew warriors back then whom for some odd reason are in my life now. If that is not odd their names are the same. They smell the same, fight the same, look the same. It appears we change lives but not appearances.

The village was down the bottom of the hill had many large buildings added even the monastery was being changed this strange red dressed man had come from the church with the power to change everything he had only been here a few weeks half the landowners even high-born families had been charged with heresy and worst still witchery.

If it were proved the church took everything lands titles silver leaving them dead or destitute. This Bishop was a cruel self-serving beast it was not long after William had been made king still Saxons were rebelling. Up the North end of the country in parts of Yorkshire were many such men.

I was a high-born Saxon lady before the battle in 1066 I had three brothers plus a father, we held lands that supported most of the Village. My mother had sadly died but not before teaching me all about herbs tinctures resins and making creams, lotions to heal the sick and heal battle wounds. She taught me how to help women in childbirth on this day 1070. I was called to come to some Christian woman who was new here, she was struggling to give birth. I took what I needed headed there with my maid Bryson the baby was not head down she was rather weak I told her we could manipulate her womb to get the baby to turn she nodded. We both started to try move her child, it worked a few hours later she gave birth to a healthy 8lb baby boy. I tended her stitched her up applied cream to help her heal staunch the blood I tended the child added a powdered herb to help his cord heal bathed him dressed him gave him his mother. I gave her a tea of lavender chamomile and vervain to help her to sleep.

2 days pass when suddenly I am disturbed whilst tending another birthing in the village, the Bishop and the girl's family had objected to my stitching up the woman and using herbal treatments, he claimed it was evil witchery. Bryson and I Igraine ran as fast as we could to my horses, we rode like the wind to see the new Lord. towards the castle the place was so busy with all the work. I grabbed a man's arm where is your lord please, we must see him. They took us into the large room a man who was tall with long dark hair stood over some maps with some men I begged to be heard they had only let me in because I was high born. I told him about our problem he nodded talked Two of his men they took my belt bag and pouch the man smelt them he said its wormwood and vervain my lord. Silver she has a lot, the other things are rags and lavender chamomile and a tincture my lord she could be a Witch indeed lock them up till I find out what is going on in this dam place. He had fought with William was close to him hence being granted Saxon lands we know not what became of the family. We were dragged away put down in the old cellars. Guarded by two men drinking ale and demolishing pie. They talked about rounding up rebels to take to the king, laughing about the difference between Saxon and Norman ladies. One danced about holding two bowls as breasts saying Saxons do not mix the blood line. They have boobies like coconuts wear their head covered when married but loose when

single. Our ladies are finer but smaller less on the hips and thighs buts in the other one. I like a bit of flesh get a grip of. What the use of snagging a bony arsed wench, when you can choose a bit of some at hold onto. Much better shag anyway. So, you tried it then, hell yes have not you go down that tavern in that village get thee self a real woman. Aye I might give it a go, I quiet fancy that one, she looks OK to me. Touch it the lord will have your head. The other is OK it is just a servant.

Sometime later I was taken out of this place brought back up to the hall, my hair now loose down my back, my dress dirty from the floor. The place had a lot of soldiers in there a few noblemen plus this bishop and the girl's family. I was pushed to my knees as a guard said you kneel before our Lord. The Norman knight said the Bishop charges you with heresy and witchery what say you? I said I is no witch or heretic my lord I am the local healer. I tends women in childbirth this family were not there when I tended the young woman recently arrived here. The child was stuck as he was laying wrong had I left this woman her and the child would now be dead the family grieving their loss instead, they have a grandson and a daughter who will heal well. I my lord can stitch up and dress battle wounds, heal many maladies and cure other hurts too. But I am no witch or heretic because the church like to use this word to remove a person's wealth the Bishop is now a rich man, he has been destroying our landed population by accusing females of being a witch, then hanging them without trial to gain their property. Should not that land have gone to the King.

He turns to the bishop is this true, he stammers they were practicing pagan ways lord forbidden by law. Why did I not get to hear of these hangings? He speaks to his men says go to the village I want names family who have been accused land that has been taken assessed for worth yes lord

Then he says to me I has heard your reasons for the use of these herbs you carry. I declare you are not guilty of witchery. I would like to speak to your father will you come with me or ride alone. I said I ride alone my horse is outside.

We attend my father this Norman lord proposes that if he were to marry me the Bishop could never harm me again, that he could use a healer in the castle should this be acceptable your land will be protected too. My father turned to me yes I agrees, she will wed you at Lammas. I say I will not do such a thing wed a stranger and Norman. You will obey your father. Knowing I was now to be his wife and chattel as under their law's women were owned by the man had no rights of their own. Under Saxon law a woman could inherit property. I was wed at Lammas; the feast was strange with Saxon at one table Norman is at another the bedding ceremony over with. The following morning, we leave for his land no but 4 miles away. He takes me to a nice room upstairs down a stone narrow corridor a new addition. The fire is lit a chair and a bed in the room. My chest is brought up, he comes up with two servants both Saxons. He throws my dresses at them keep them she will not be wearing them I will have new made. A woman measures me comes with silk, linen and wool cloth. I choose the colours that is all. I spend near on a month in my night shift, up in that room. Only seeing him once per day. When he decides to call in at all that is. Once I had dresses I could go out, but not unescorted I wanted go the woods, but the guards said I could not leave his orders you understand. So, Bryson who did not dwell at the castle but in the village came each day I had not seen my father for months. So, I asked her to swop clothing she could stay in my rooms claiming not very well. She ought not open the door to anyone. I then walked freely out of the castle to the village picking herbs once away. I visited my father who was extremely sick. I think I fell asleep because when I woke it was dawn. I headed back to the castle they let me in but as I walked to the great hall, my lord was there he grabbed me saying where have you been dressed like this. I told him. Go to your rooms and wash I will talk with you later. I went to Bryson she had a bruise on her face I asked her what happened. She said I told the servants I was not well did not want dinner. But later your lord came to the room he went ballistic demanding to know where you were. He has been pacing the castle he sent men to seek you. After this my lord told his guards I under no circumstances was to leave without an escort. That Bryson was now to remain with her lady.

The Lords men return with news they have calculated the value of land seized by the bishop and hidden over just four months he had been here 10 families were charged he even hung the children. The Lord had him brought here, he said lady you will attend me. I need you to see how justice is dispensed here. The bishop and his retinue are brought in. The bishop swearing before god he was doing holy work nothing wrong at all. Witness after witness was brought to swear statement that none were witches only that their land bordered his. He wanted more as he grew wealthy these people had died on false charges before evidence was produced.

The bishop said he did not answer to this lord, but to the pope of Rome. My lord laughed said but right now you are on my land in my jurisdiction and have broken the king's laws evidence must be proven before a hanging. Now all land is seized in the name of the king. Lock them up on the morrow they can be put on a ship back to Rome. The very next day Bryson and I were coming down the staircase when my lord said hold lady stay there. He had a young lad against the wall he said when I say bring my sword I mean now boy, next time you take forever I will slit you from gizzard to neck.

Flash forward to present well to 1993 New Year's Eve I am at a party man drinking ale from my boots. A man rides past on a blue motorbike

I hit Gaza an Wolfs saying he is the one he is the one. How I knew I did not question. Week passes by had moved into my new house, I attend karate grading's he is there in the line taking his blue belt I my orange.

He leaves straight after his as kids are near his bike, another week we walk into karate at a new club there standing with the sensei is him. My daughter says this time talk to him; say you do not know the Kata for green belt yet ask for help. That is how we met in this life. Now he was Mark. After he has moved in, we go buy a solid oak bed. It was delivered in the afternoon; the men were to build it in the room. I had called Allen my gay friend from university. To me he was a girl, but he was most definitely a boy, as Allen and I are trying out my bed, Mark arrives at the back garden on his bike.

Within minutes he had a spear at Allen's throat, I was saying hey stop this look at our new bed, thinking he was jesting. But the voice was not mark it was that of my Norman lord, he turned to me said Lady I will deal with you later he said prey tell me boy what are you doing in my lady's bed chamber.? The spear was right into Allen's throat, I, was worried he might hurt him. But at that moment a video of the scene on the stairs in the castle played out before my eyes. Now I knew where I knew Allen from 1070. Mark suddenly came back, said what is wrong? I said you nearly killed Allen, do not be daft come on let us get a drink. I had the weirdest dream you know that I had a sword at his throat on the stairs of the castle we lived in. Yes, I said so did I.

One day mark brings home bunches of thin metal then he takes an old kitchen draw, pushes a metal rod through it then bends a handle. He sits winding coils on this rod then cutting the coils into links to make chain mail he made a coif and a shirt the shirt is big and weighs around

56lbs. I said how did you know how make all that well he replies I was a lord of a castle and a good fighter.

So, memories leak through

Whispers of the Witch by NanyWytch

April 2002 suspected poltergeist

249 copyright Ashna Yates BSC 2020

Whispers of the Witch by NanyWytch

It began just after Ostaria in Biddulph a toy rag doll took on the manifestation of something a voice spoke from it. The cradle of filth poster had a child's face appear in it; things went missing then appeared later that same day somewhere else often in garden. Both girls had been attacked by something unseen dragged about the room had hair pulled been physically held by feet and dangled. The family dog became so terrified it chewed off its own leg. It had to have surgery now it refused come into the house lived in z kennel in the garden.

Loud pacing was heard upstairs, shadows seen in the hall, the family moved the doll and poster to the shed. That is when the banging started on the shed walls. In the house the pressure dropped rapidly it became ice cold.

4 members of my coven witnessed these events plus 2 friends. We went to pick up the girl things cantered around as soon as she was in the car the car became ice cold in seconds

Abbey suffered from depression and anxiety took pills for it, she and her sister had been badly abused by the elder brother. Abbey had just started her blood time at 13 years old. Her father being African blamed Abbey for the abuse his son could do no wrong he beat Abbey calling her a whore. He had since returned to Somalia. Leaving the girls in the care of their alcoholic mother and violent brother.

History of case.

12 months prior to these disturbing things occurring in the house Abbey and her friend had been reading stuff on the net about magic they decided do a ritual from a book her friend had bought they chose to do it in a graveyard at the church they were both of African descent. They did Ouija in the graveyard and called on some deity from the

book. It took place at 9pm in the dark moon at St Lawrence Church in Biddulph

Told by Abbey

It went cold I felt very strange and weird not like me at all but something odd had happened to me we sat down drank some wine we blessed gave some to the earth. Then we called on something it came it threw the planchete away from us we got scared and ran away but I still felt very odd I was being sick, couldn't sleep couldn't do stuff couldn't remember things then my nana who loved me died and mother got worse she was drunk all the time. Abbey said I made myself better by cutting my arms when the blood flowed it was like the bad was coming out of me .

Abbey became obsessed with her sisters baby as she had moved out of the house into her own place with her boyfriend. After Abbey came round a lot we got attacked it was taking place at 15 Williams avenue Biddulph we went to the house with Jack and Damon

Steph is fully aware of some presence in her sister she feels she cannot hug her at all as it will not let her when she tried hug abbey she was thrown across the floor . Reading of the picture of the brother showed us he was now older than this picture there was a shadow person standing right behind him there was a red line around his neck like he had been strangled yet he was still alive

Abbey relied on her cuddles with the baby for comfort. As she got no love from anywhere else. Abbey claimed she was attacked at the graveyard by something dead. We did a cleansing of the house persuaded Abbey she needed some psychological help from the mental health team once in hospital things in the house went back to normal. The spirit that had attached itself to Abbey had now gone.

Abbey needed care the disturbances were her cry for help really and this attached spirit had helped do this

Abbey is now in Foster care and thriving very well she has counselling for the abuse her brother was arrested and sent down.

So sometimes it is not magic that is needed sometimes its medical help.

Guides

I have decided end my book with a chapter about guides. This is how I contacted mine

Physically we contain both the x & y chromosome both male and female energies are within us our Anima /Animus are the opposite to our biological nature. Magick requires both these energies in balance we must meet our other self.

Lay down in a comfortable place take 3 very deep breaths to fill your lungs breathe out very slowly watch the rise and fall of your breathe.

Now visualise a cave before you, now walk into it take the lantern from Hecate as she offers it go up the stone steps into the room above, look around there are only two other doors here one leads out to a ledge where you can view the stars enjoy the night sky and the moons light . Go back inside find a seat to sit on now call your guide toward you do not rush do it and wait your guide will come through the other door

When they do ask questions their name where they were from how they know you. Get to know what they look like so you are aware of them ask for a sign just between you that you can use to call them.

I know this works as it's how I met mine he is a pure-bred Celt more priest than warrior he had a sign we use as I cannot pronounce his name properly, he doesn't mind over the years we have come to know each other well. He has a sense of humour and he swears sometimes but he is a good teacher of things we have these wonderful conversations now I can ask anything he will reply

So, try it out write down everything you can recall keep this notebook just for your guides conversations if you learn how to do automated writing it makes there passing on knowledge easier it does feel a bit odd but use blank sheets paper and a pen sit down allow your guide use your arm but they can write very fast indeed it matters not when you get your arm back you can read it and write it in your book. It does not matter if you do not understand what they talk about you can ask them to help you but by keeping a record you will have this you look back on in years to come. These two amazingly simple things have helped me out a lot over the year's guides can be funny too it is not all serious

Once the contact is fully established you will have someone you can rely on be very truthful. What you need to understand is there is no black magic unless you mean the chocolates of course. It is the mind of the person that dictates if an intention is dark or light. Having said this, we all have a darker side. Plus, we all have roots, we came from the dark because all life is created in the dark of the womb of mother.

So please stop thinking in the way the church does that anything they do not understand is the devil's work. There is no such creature on our path in order to come in contact with this devil you must first be Christian and believe it is real. Now Satan and Lucifer are not this creature. They are Angelic forms.

Now to help beginners out I has put these questions to ask your guide.

1. Who are you?
2. Where are you from
3. How do you know me?
4. Why are you my guide
5. Name you prefer to be called
6. How do I call you?
7. Is there a sign we can make between just us?
8. What do you do in your spare time?

Once you get to know them, they ought to be your first point of contact about yourself and your magic path.

I suggest you have 3 notebooks

1, for dreams

1. for book of days
2. For any magical rituals & spells

Your book of days is for everything including meditations or daily practice record how you felt before the intention of the work how you felt during whom you met talked to how you felt afterwards. Make sure you protect yourself and banish afterwards.

Children will play.

Bringing up your children as pagans gives them other views on things, they learn considerably basic things whilst young. Tanith came home one day furious about some teacher who had made a comment about her being pagan. She asked what can I do to help me feel better do you know what scares her? Yes, spiders there is your answer. Oh, I get it she said the next day the same teacher was being awful to her again, so Tanith asked come to see her about a word she did not understand. Whilst at the desk she dropped spider down her blouse went sit down. Minutes later the teacher was jumping about screaming, she would not touch the spider, she just screamed and jumped about. The children were laughing, Tanith walked unto the teacher took the spider said oops sorry I must have dropped him.

The teacher never said another word to Tanith that was about her being pagan.

But sometimes children will experiment with dangerous things for the young are prone to ignoring the rules. One night we got a phone call from the children's father he said he needed my help as morgana had called something up in her room and he could not get into her. That things were banging and clattering around the house. So, we came to Macclesfield at around 7pm, up to then mark had been in open circle and rituals but not seen what I do first-hand. So, we called it his real initiation.

When we arrived, Mike was upstairs with Mythrynn on landing as we stood talking about what had occurred a light bulb unscrewed itself very slowly then it floated slowly to the floor before smashing against the wall. Mark jumped back how is this possible? Its playing I said trying scare us well its working said Mark then the banging moved to downstairs the men went down there to get into the lounge, but the door would not open, nor the one to the kitchen. Mark is a big guy he was puzzled about the doors. Meanwhile I had gone to the bedroom pushed into the room the wardrobe had been moved to behind the door. My daughter was floating a few inches off the bed. Whatever it was laughed as it open and shut the draws saying you cannot hurt me as mothers will not hurt their own baby. I said put her down right now it said she is out right now but will say you called round. I was amused but then knew what I was dealing with. I said to Mike run the bath for me consecrate the water and use this rock salt put that in we need wash the dirt off our baby ok he said I said seal the stairs so it cannot leave that way. Call on Michael to help you. He knew exactly what to do I knew he would do it. I returned to the bedroom walked up to my child picked her up, it said hey what you doing witch? Going give my child a bath she is dirty.

It did not understand what I was up to as it was such a low-level thing, I placed morgana fully clothed into the bath the thing screamed out you tricked me no am washing my baby as she has attracted dirt onto her. Tricky but I am still, here yes I said you are submerged my daughters head for a few seconds then pulled her up the thing had come out of her but was in the room. My daughter was back sobbing wanting hugs she kept saying the book said it would be OK, but it was not OK am sorry.

I said to the thing floating about the room you have two ways out that I can see one is that way pointing to Michael the other is inside this egg that I will take outside it chose to go into the egg. I took it outside dug a small hole placed the egg into it then added rock salt and earth the weight broke the egg. Problem solved.

We went back home on the way Tanith said now you have seen how mum works you are ok yeah he said but that thing about the doors. I said sometimes energy can be used to make you think something is locked when it is not so what was it? A low-level larval thing had no place being in our world at all. Tanith said so it went into the egg because the arch angel would be nice yes but when you put the salt and earth on top would that not break the egg yes darling so it was scrambled yes plus it couldn't get out the salt and earth would contain it. So magic is about looking at something from a logical viewpoint and deciding what way is best

Sometimes a problem is easy to solve other time it is a bit harder but once you know what you are doing it gets easier. Plus, not everyone would want to clean up other people's mess the only reason I did most of them was I knew the local people they all knew I was a witch as I did not hide it.

Whispers of the Witch by NanyWytch

Dead flowers

What happened here I never wish to see again because if the gods abandon you nothing will be good for you.

Our coven had grown everyone got along as we had an open circle where candidates came for a year and a day before they could come into the coven. This way they got to know us, we them nearer the end of their year they would be invited to a seasonal sabot. Then the existing members all got a vote on if they would say yeah or nay. That is how ours worked. We are a hierarchical coven we teach you from the very beginning.

one day I am busy cleaning house when I heard sobbing from outside, opening my back door I see scouse one of our male witches. Pulling him inside asking what is wrong why he is so upset his answer got me very puzzled. He said right now your boyfriend is in bed with my wife. I said come on take me to yours but first I will ring where he works to say he left his wallet at home. So, I make the call am told he had been sacked 3 month ago as some female kept coming interrupted his work.

So, we go to scoucers House he let me in said do not step on third step it creaks but first door on left its open a bit. I go up and yes, they were in the bed and were having sex my boyfriend bare backside was right there. She was moaning but just before the climax I opened the door, coughed said morning am I disturbing you? Interesting question this but erg how long this has been going on for as your both meant to be at work.

Would 3 months be about right Julie as for the last 3 full moons you were suddenly unwell. Now I know that Paul is not craft and normally goes out with mates on coven nights to the pub. Plus I know he got sacked from work 3 months ago.

He jumps up it is not like; you think she means nothing it is just sex she offered so I did not turn it down. After all we are not that serious are we? We just live together

Right is that so well might I suggest you get dressed because there is an irate husband downstairs. What he is here yes darling how do you think I got into your house.

He is never home at this time ever,

Well today he is

Once downstairs the husband and wife talk or shout in the kitchen whilst we talk in the lounge I was very calm indeed, I simply said he was moving out today if what we had is that unimportant. Scouse came out the kitchen said can I come stay at yours, I am not sleeping here with her. She can keep him.

So, we left them at her house we went to mine, scoucers was more concerned about his two children than himself. He said he wanted a divorce, and he wanted go for custody of his girls. That night we ate steak with a lovely mushroom sauce and sliced potatoes he was a chef, so the food was great. We also downed a bottle of red each. The next day scouse phoned in saying he needed time off so did I so we could sort out our lives.

He contacted a lawyer, I decided get rid of stuff I did not want to keep because they reminded me of him. I packed his stuff up called him to say his shit was on the garden. Now between us we had 2 vans 3 cars. 4 motorbikes most did not work he said he would fix them but that was a year ago. Now as he was not going to be here I decided to sell them after all I had bought them. So, I called a scrap guy said come make me an offer he did I accepted £2000 for vans,£1000 for the cars &£ 1000 for the bikes that were mostly scrap except one. I wanted a clean slate I spilt the money in half put his in an envelope with a note I sold all the shit.

Now issue being that as man and wife they had both entered the coven at the same time. But these last 3 moons she had failed to attend scouse worked out he would have been with her that night till well up to midnight whilst he was out. So, we asked the rest of the coven what they thought we ought to do? As I said everyone got a vote about people in the coven, we had a grievance policy where any member could discuss a problem with us either privately or in coven. Scoucers wanted it in full, coven. So, we called an esbat meeting, on new moon for new beginnings.

The coven voted she needed to be there given her explanation for the 3 missed rituals if her husband attended saying the girls were with their grandma that night.

So, he called her said he would arrange for the girl go his mums he would take them after school so she could come to coven. At this point I felt a bit sorry for her. As she had no idea the coven all knew about her affair. That the general consensus was they simply wanted her clarification as to why she had not attended coven. After all our rules were simple if you could not make it you phoned to say so. You did not just leave us wondering you see her problem was she had been at work during the day as she worked as my secretary, so I knew she was not

Sick. At the meeting she admitted that she was having an affair and that the last 3 moons she had been with him at a hotel. So now the coven decided that she was to leave the coven. That she would be banished from it and not have communication with us. Excepting her current husband if he wanted to.

Few months later I bump into her in town she looked rather upset, so being a nice person, I asked her sit down have a coffee with me. She accepted we chatted she had just lost custody of girls to him. Who had arranged the children's nana would mind them whilst he was at work? I said that I did feel sorry for her that had happened asked what grounds she said neglect. I was a bit shocked because she had been a good mum. But it seems when the judge talked to the children mummy was too busy to make tea, or breakfast for them now daddy was staying at my house. They said she had forgot get them from school. So, nana had come, and they stayed there rather than at home because mummy was too busy now in bed.

I comforted her till she was ok she walked away them a few minutes later came back with a bunch of flowers she said give these to the goddess for me. I took them but seconds later they had rotted in my hand so badly they were slimy dropped them looked up and my expression was pure shock I had never seen Anything like this before. I took a very deep breath and thought wow the goddess refused the flowers quick.

I talked to the coven who simply said well she broke her oath to the gods; she treated her children badly and destroyed her marriage guess they abandoned her.

Our Gods can be very nice to us, but please never make one mad, and never break a oath sworn before them.

The Vision

I had a vision of two pyramids side by side guarded by serpents and a seal over the door inside this burial chamber were a priest of asset and a priestess of Isis lay at right angles to each other in their hands they both held a gold disc. They had golden masks over their faces. I seemed to have semblance of form in this vision to enter the body of the priestess as I knew it was myself in there. I talked to the Priest who seemed to be there as well. We were to prevent the discs being taken. As it was thought humans were not to have the knowledge contained in them. The vision ended as two people in 1930s clothing were in the chamber, they were trying to remove the lids to the burial sarcophagus. When black snakes came from the sand biting them, they died at the side of this The Egyptian guide would not enter past the doorway. He lived he did not break the seal.

Later with research I discovered this vision was all about me and the high priest who had given up his life for me. The snake figure over the entrance was TZ in other texts just Z. the date of the burial was 2670BC or 4655 years ago in the second dynasty period. In the region of Khet-seken-way which ended in 2660BC

At this time, the two lands were gaining peace after a time of political and religious strife. The capital had moved from Abydos to Memphis. The location of the tomb was in CIDEK it is not on the maps. The occupants of this tomb were a Priest of Asset and Isis aged 39 years and a priestess of Ishtar & Isis aged 22 both were Egyptians the name of the female was Ayesha the name of the male was Durgapur.

Events leading to their deaths was a result of them falling in love when he visited the temple each month, they had secretly had an affair with each other culminating in them have sex in the temple of the dark Isis.

In the temple of Asset, the priests did not have to remain pure but in the temple of Ishtar and Isis the females were to remain pure as sacrifices to the goddess.

It was judged they should be killed without burial rites, but because He gave his life freely when he did not have to, they decided we would have burial rites hence all the decorations on our bodies,

For me, this answered lots of questions I had about a memory of being given to the temple at aged 5 years as my parents could not afford give over a sheep. The high Priest had suggested they gave me instead, it was the custom to bring gift to the temples at each month's rituals but to b ring a sacrifice on the feast days.

I lived inside the temple was taught everything till I became a priestess we would dance at the celebrations I still know this dance and I met two others from that life here in today's time I met with a girl I knew back then as Asker and the priest I was buried with in this life his name is Peter, he attended my initiation

priestess in this life.

This chapter is about a past life of mine and how I died in that life. I had memories of that life that until the vision I did not understand. Now I know my vision and memories are true.

Another world forms

Other world form is Astral body for example once you have learnt to go out of your body you can go anywhere you wish but walking the paths, we tend to go to further our knowledge. I would go frequently to the library of Alexandria where my teacher would take me places to learn things about spirit. It made things much better for me this chapter is about meeting Lucifer for the first time. I was cleaning up in my temple it was the full moon rite later that day. I was checking we had what we needed in our supply cupboard, as I needed to clean out the coal fire grate, I placed 3 rings in silver box on the altar we normally kept moon incense in here, so it had that smell. My rings were safe in there or so I thought. I continued my cleaning, then realised we had no moon incense left in our cupboard draws, I stood at the altar I had stripped to reset for the moon rites working out in my head if I could make something appropriate from stocks of herbs and resins. Whilst I was puzzling this out in my head, we had frankincense, myrrh, birch bark, plenty of other types of incense but nothing except ritual oil then I noticed two people had appeared near my dark mirror standing in the North gate. I said hello who are you? What do you want? One of them spoke said our Lord sent us with a gift for you. He hands me a gold necklace in a box, I said whom is your Lord why is he sending gifts to me? Our Lord is Lucifer, he says tell you he has watched you grow and wishes very much to meet and converse with you over a meal. So, he is inviting me to dinner, yes Lady but he wishes you to accept this token. I said I cannot accept the gift as I cannot give a gift back. Lady my lord does not want a gift just to meet you. I said take that back tell him invitations are best delivered face to face. Yes Lady, they were gone.

Less than 10 minutes had past I opened the box to find my rings missing, I knew where I had put them, but I still looked around in case

I had dropped them when changing the whole altar cloth for the silver one. Suddenly the two were back again they were tall, they looked human enough, but I knew they were servitors of his. Themselves. Lower level, demons, I said what now.? The taller one spoke this time Lady my Lord was distressed you didn't want the gold chain, so instead he offers this for you to wear they open the box show me this most beautiful dress I had ever seen, it was red with sparkles all sewn into the dress the material was red satin it flowed very well there were red gloves to match the dress and a fur stole. I loved it but in my mind was the talk my magus had had with me the weekend before about how easy it is for you to lose your soul. The Lord of light now being in charge on earth after being refused re-entrance to heaven. You must remember that what we call demons were once angels who defied gods' instructions to destroy humans. Instead, they taught us all the sciences and music. They taught humans about gold and jewels, where to obtain them. Without there teachings we would indeed be primitive. Even though I often think we behave as if we were Neanderthal towards each other.

I said please tell your Lord thank you for taking the time to offer this dress, but I will choose my own, please tell him I accept his kind offer to meet with him. The taller demon said yes, my Lady we will come fetch you at midnight in otherworld form. They were gone. I opened the silver box which had my rings in it and was now full of moon incense, I smelt it thinking well I do not care where it came from, we can use it later.

Our Rites to Diana went very well one of our coven witches had written a speech for the full moon, we still use today. My lady came through so strong my whole voice sounded unlike me, she told me I would be safe not to concern myself with fears that were unrealistic.

After copious amounts of wine, the coven bed down for the night I lie down in my bed and go out of my body return to my temple room, at midnight the two I met earlier came to fetch me. I went with them they took me to a large building more like a castle with many floors. At the entrance they said Lady your dress, I had forgotten to dress, they gave me the red sparkling dress, I put it on the one hand me a crown for my head of jewels I was wearing my Amber & jet necklace my temple rings. The dress looked absolutely brilliant. They showed me myself in the mirror, then gave me silver slippers to wear saying a gift from your goddess lady. They open this huge door, in front of me were two long line of Demons ranging from low to high. I walked down this line noticing them bow their heads to me. Then as I neared this higher raised area with four steps which resembled a semi-circular dais. 6 of the higher ranked demons stepped in front of me guarding their Lord. I stood there said your Lord invited me here move. They looked at their Lord who nodded and they moved to the sides, they were staring at me it was a little uncomfortable, I walk up the steps to him who is now standing before me. He is a very handsome man blonde hair that is quiet long but the eyes they were the brightest blue eyes I have ever seen pale skin beautiful complexion. He is tall and muscular a girl could just go there. Yes, he had a cute bum too. We walk away together he tells them they are dismissed the hall clears in seconds. It was like the turned and vanished right before us.

We go into a room with a lovely fireplace the fire blazing in its hearth logs piled up at the side, a huge table with just two seats at the top end laid out with silver tableware, goblets, flowers serviettes. It all looked genuinely nice, we sat down at the table he clapped his hand two servers brought out food roast lamb, roast chicken, lots of different vegetables and potatoes. He said I know you like these meats but did not know which vegetables you preferred so we have a good selection. We ate as we chatted at first about Diana, the fact she knew where I was as he had spoken with her about meeting me as I have said before Gods have their own rules to follow which means Lucifer would need her consent to meet a servitor belonging to her. She had acknowledged his need and agreed to this meeting provided he escorts me home himself. Before dawn when the gates close

By this I refer to the fact the darker forces work more at night but as Dawn approaches, they must all go home because if not they will be trapped in the light. Till sunset. So now you know where the story about vampires comes from about them being allergic to light. Demons are not allergic to light but do much prefer to work at night out of the suns glare.

Many fairy stories are very real like red riding Hood meeting a wolf, now this may not have been a wolf but a very charming gentleman with eyebrows that meet in the middle for they are furry on the inside and ought to be avoided whereas wolves who are wolves do not have eyebrows. The real fairy stories were not like they are today very tapered down versions but written or told as lessons. You need recall that most people over time did not read nor write everything was given in stories passed down the line.

Lucifer was exceedingly kind we talked about the light bearer and him being the strongest angel there was the best warrior and that God was very arrogant bad tempered and selfish. That he lied all, the time used the angels badly, to fight his wars as they were created as his army. that next to him Michael was the strongest warrior, that they were all brothers. But those who had walked away from God, took care of their own. These were all higher-level angels the best he had that were warriors. But they defied his wishes when they actually met humans. Finding they were given things the angels were denied. Humans had emotions and the ability to choose what they wanted to do. Whereas Angels were not granted these things so many were jealous that god gave them more. Made them better than Angels who had no free will, no emotions, no choices in what they did when or how they were tied to just obeying. It caused this huge revolt against God. When over 300 of his best turned away from him taking Lucifer as their Lord.? Lucifer was the next angel in power to God these angels chose to remain on earth it was not that they were banned from going home, they simply decided to stay. Create their own place here. There is a hierarchy here as there was with God, the higher Angels made the rules and enforced them.

Lucifer talked about light and darkness being in balance that I needed to ensure I did not just learn the path of light but also the path of the dark to balance out my knowledge. He said he would help me, but I needed to learn the language of the Angels before he could really teach me as speaking in our language did not sit well for them teaching me about their own paths. That he was incredibly happy I had come to know his brother Michael well. Along with the fact I had met Azrael as well.

That both the light and darkness would aid me now. If I called, they would come. He escorted me back to my home, kissed my head like a father would wish me good night told me to get a good rest start again on the morrow. I slept deeply dreamt about Diana talking to him sharing a walk in her woods.

I was in a quandary about adding this into the book, but I think others might find it impossible to comprehend when they themselves are not yet as far along the path as myself. Those who are thus far or close to this far will understand how this happened. One thing I do need to say is a warning do not fall into the first trap, of the astral time is different there. What you may think is 30 minutes could be as long as 3 days. Do not ever leave your body unprotected and go wandering. Yes, it is wonderful to discover you can travel fast anywhere you desire, simply by thought. Do not ever try to alter things you see there. You may learn that as time is different on the astral you can travel back to old shells revue that life to learn why you chose to do things this way in this life.

I learnt about all my past lives this way, based on memories I had that were Incomplete. By returning to that time, I could watch myself in another life as if seeing a video today. The Akashic records have all our lives in them if you try to see them when not yet developed enough the guardian will refuse you send you away. If you break rules up there the watchers will drop kick you back into your body fast like falling off a cliff you don't want to offend the guardians if they say you have not knowledge of this place go it's a warning that you need to leave right now. You can learn a lot but do not stay away from your body, long as it needs water and food whilst you do not when in spirit form, but you can eat and drink up there. But your body must be awake to gain nourishment. Learning that you can leave your body can come as a shock as it did for me that first time. Be polite to whom you meet, talk to them ask questions. I meet my guides this way now as we can converse in a more practical way, I has an Eagle with very sharp claws and talons. Plus, my warrior /priest who has been with me since well the 5th century. Then an old woman from a village in the 8th century.

Whispers of the Witch by NanyWytch

Midsummer Madness

275 copyright Ashna Yates BSC 2020

Taken from coven notes 22nd June 1984.

These are accurate notes from the above date, initially I hesitated in placing them here, but they show how the gods work closely with us. They show how they will intercede if they feel its best.

Present were

Circe guide of souls

Cyrene assistant priest

Hekomya as sacrificed god

Adrienne candidate for initiation

Jonathan visiting priest

Nick visiting priest

Philip covener

Mike high Priest

Tanith morgana Athena the children.

Background to this night, the week prior we were meant to meet up with a person who enquired about the coven she had attended our circles for over 6 months her name now near the top it was prudent to meet her more formally. I myself with the assistant priest had gone to York to meet her. She had not turned up after 4 hours in York minster we called it a day went back home. The weekend after was our Luthra rites plus we were taking in another to our coven from another coven two of its members were present now those present on Friday had parts to play in the rites for tonight.

As we were about to begin there was a phone call Grace whom we were to meet the week before but not heard a word from. Said she was standing at our train station it was now 8pm on Friday night. The craft rules as well as heathen rules say a guest should be welcomed and given the best you have to offer. So, myself and my assistant went to meet her, it was far too late now to send her home as trains were not running from our smaller station after 9pm. So, we were getting no choice as to having bring her to our home. The girl who had attended open circle was pleasant enough which was another reason we were to meet up the week prior.

So, we were not overly worried about this, she knew us all already. At the station what we saw coming over the bridge was not that young vibrant girl but something else entirely. By something else we mean exactly that what was walking toward us was not quiet human. Maybe underneath it may well be but this awkward looking beast that munched sweets and was wearing far too much makeup. We were very puzzled this could not be grace it was only 3 moons since we had last seen her.

But here we were in this situation that clearly should not have been. Without other way but to allow her stay overnight till the trains started up again.

The following will be written straight as the notes from the coven members were written.

Adrienne

The vibrations from Grace were quiet odd there was decay and it smelt like death was sitting here or something not quiet dead but I felt pity for her although I hadn't met her before I noticed my energies were waning whereas before her admittance here my energies were fine. I felt I should talk to her because she was a lovely soul. I felt as if my life force was being sucked from me. As the time for my initiation came closer I became Even worse I think the coven members noticed as one of them came to me asking me to come sit further away. He wrapped his legs around me and held me awfully close to him. My energy peeked upwards now.

Once alone in the room with her she tried offering me sweet cakes from a bag she had refused put down. I refused saying thank you. She started to get a bit fidgety and wanted to know where the children had gone to. They had been put to bed and I know they were protected by another member of the coven Grace had not seen. She asked if there was any heating in the place I looked at the thermostat it said 17 degrees I said its on. She said she was cold, so I handed her a blanket off the sofa. I was quiet hot, and I was just wearing a silk robe belonging the high priestess. She started to shake like she was afraid of something I asked if she were OK she kept eating from thus bag and asking about the girls. She wandered up the hall towards there room but saw something on the floor outside the room that made her take her hand off the door. I was worried now for the girls, but I knew the coven would not allow anyone into them.

She started to talk incessantly her voice getting louder and louder every utterance she made, I did not understand but then the priest came out of the temple and yelled at her to be quiet or she would be spending the night at a closed train station. I thought she might cry but she did not she sat huddled in this blanket and her coat holding this bag close to her chest.

Lady Circe

Whispers of the Witch by NanyWytch

As we started to cast the circle the noise kept getting louder the whole coven wondered who was making this odd throbbing intonations. The high priest walked out told Grace to shut up,

Guide of souls, I had to fetch the candidate into the temple guide her as the two officiating priests were running this rite, our assistant priest had cast the circle he was to assist the high priest as part of his tests for 3rd level. Once robed in the guide of souls costume nobody would know whom it was within it, the skull mask obscured all the face the gloves the hands. I tied our candidate in the prescribed way watching the thing huddled like a bag in the corner it feared me why I did not then know. I had to entrust my 3 girls to Philip a member of the coven who had been asleep prior to Grace arriving he said to us what an earth is that it is not our grace not that. Why is it here? He would not come into the lounge, so he had been given the job of protecting the children.

During the rite, my concentration fleeting between the realms and outside where I sensed great danger was lurking. I knew grace had opened the door to the children's room 3 times as my guardian told me where she was. She did not go inside had she tried she would have been escorted off the property. I felt something was trying to gain entrance to their room. But we had protected it from the outside. Inside was more protection placed because of this odd situation

Adrienne

I felt safe inside the circle even though I could not see but suddenly I felt a sense of urgency and the clairvoyance came through, I said Do not leave it without danger great danger will unfold this night protect them protect them.

I was past a lot of power and I felt extraordinarily strong now, them there was the hilarity as the priest said he could not find my knees. I had managed to keep the robe on I guess the guide of souls attention had been diverted as I was meant to be naked. We laughed and they simply got on with the rite moving the gown out the way.

Philip

As soon as I saw Grace I thought yuk what's that doing here it wasn't the grace, we had been in open circle with my eyes weren't deceiving me she creeped me out so I volunteered stay with the 3 girls to give them lessons in how to seal a room how to protect each other Tanith was a fast learner so was Morgana. Of course, the baby was far too young, but the girls kept saying there is a bad creature outside our door do not let it in here it is an unbelievably bad monster. I said I would attend Luthra as I knew I could set things in motion protect the girls. After the initiation, the high priest said we need talk about what is happening here and if we ought to change things to make sure we are present. But everyone wanted to do Luthra not wait till the next night. So, they voted on if Grace should be brought into the temple to be watched rather than risking her being without.

We had been told by the gods that someone was clinging to life when in actual fact they were not alive at all. We did not understand what they referred to even though we were aware of the existence of beings who would do anything to enjoy life again even taking others life force to do so. I did not want to bring it inside our temple, but everyone has a vote we abide by that vote. It was voted to bring her inside which meant it was up to me to prepare her.

Once outside the temple I checked on the girls Tanith and morgana had fell asleep together, Phil was also squashed on the bed with them with a book still in his hands. It seemed wrong to disturb them. So, I sealed the room again and went to get grace. I told her she was to join us inside and as such she needed to undress and wear a robe and white cord. She went to the bathroom to change we had no locks on doors because when smaller one of the girls had locked themselves inside a room and we had broken a window to get inside.

I picked up it thought it was winning a battle that we yet knew nothing about, there was malice and yet fear as well. I made excuse to enter the room saying I was desperately in need of a pee. I was not I just wanted to see Grace or this creature covering grace. She had undressed she had no feet just these half rotten decaying blocks of something that once were feet. She looked grey like she was dead and decaying not pink and flowing with life force. I did not quite know what had happened to our grace, but this was not her at all. This was something no longer human. There was an incredibly young soul present under far too many masks the soul was trapped in a kind of web of the abyss. I had never considered that death was like a big hole forever hungry. The threads were like a spider's web clinging to the soul devouring it bit by bit. I have never seen a live body decay like this. This person was dead spiritually but not physically yet. I pulled her to the edge of the circle it froze in a big solid mass. But we were not leaving it out there to get into the children, as Philip had come in with me helping get grace inside, we knew inside she could not function as there would be too much power. So, the plans it had would fail we all thought something was after a younger body to dwell inside hence its need get near the young girls. I was like this hawk with huge talons I grabbed it brought her inside. Mike was behaving oddly he had voted against it as had one other. He did the invocation to the goddess in a silly voice, I stared at him without saying a word if looks could kill. These were those. The goddess came in great power it was hard to contain she looked at the south gate wherein grace was sat. The rest of the invocation were done the God form came and was genuinely nice, Diana liked this person. They danced well the ladies dance was vibrant but the men's dance with the shapeshifting was brilliant

At the second female dance we decided grace shouldn't just sit that she was here so she would participate in our rites we pulled her up erriene and I to dance as we held hands I felt its crawling flesh, we placed it between us nothing can fight this raw female power as I had a goddess in me.my hand felt like something cut into me I pulled away there my ring had bent into my hand. I asked Hekomya to get it out. He did lick my hand with his tongue staring into my eyes as he did he whispered to me. We must get rid of it before it spreads its sickness within. As our rite progressed and the shape-shifting dance began, each transformation seemed better than the one before stronger more vibrant even to the writhing on the floor of our assistant priest. We forgot about the lump of decaying flesh in the south it was going nowhere guarded by Michael. We enjoyed our rite very much indeed it is my favourite of the whole year. I had turned into a coiled serpent, ready to strike but it was not the time.

Adrienne

When we danced making grace take our hands it felt like dragging a stone on a cord around with us I sensed suppressed fear yet a curiosity as well. I could not feel grace the young soul I saw crying all I could feel was something powerfully hungry lurking there. We let it crawl back to the corner it was not doing anything just watching but we grew more powerful as the rite moved onwards. It was so beautiful I knew that nick and John from my previous coven enjoyed this rite.

Cyrene

I blocked out the thing in the corner knowing later we would have to sort it out or get rid of it. For now, I just wanted be the God form that was invoked into me he was powerful I found myself being able to shape-shifting more readily than before at this rite. It was as if he knew in advance what was next in the song,

Circe

I could not really give 100% to the rite as I wanted this thing out of my temple I needed get it gone whereas, yet I did not know the Gods were here so relaxed some knowing we were safe for now. But I really wanted dig a big hole push it in stamp earth on top of it. There were many forces here of the darker world simply watching what was occurring here. We closed it down as we were leaving the temple it spoke for the first time to us. I thought the children would come I wanted to see the children are they coming join us now. No I snapped not in your presence they are safe. It laughed this sort of heinous giggle. I heard a child cry I was there in an instant Tanith said mummy a monster kept coming to our door, but we did not let it in we sealed it here. Morgana said it is a bad monster mummy it wants our baby sister, it wants to steal her away we won't let it will we. I said no we have dealt with monsters before do you want come play with us don't go near grace but stay with daddy yes can we taste the wine too. Ok I said and eat food with us. Yeah but mummy the monster will, be there, yes I said but if you stay with the men you will be safe remember they are warriors and your daddy will not let anything harm you at all. They were happier so I carried Athena in her Moses basket into the kitchen placing her on the table with a circle about her. Plus, coveners were in and out of there refilling glasses. We offered grace wine she took it drank it in fact she drank like a fish. Tipping a glass of wine straight back down her throat. She ate a lot of food too but then kept eating more from the bag she was holding. I played a game with the girls, with the hood, they came to me peeked inside its Tanith said mummy it is not you, but I put my fingers to my lips said shhhhhhhhh do not say whom it is out loud. My darling yes goddess she said laughing. Morgan looked under the hood and ran off to her dad, saying mummy gone mummy gone now snakes hiding. She was not sure whether hug me or tell me go away.

Then that incessant chatter began again coming from grace getting louder and louder like the whole house was vibrating with the noise. I put a wall between it and us, it was heard but could not do anything much. The coveners said is it time yet? L said soon do not worry we will get to relax very soon.

Adrienne said she felt odd like something was inside her, crawling inside her, whilst Mike and Phil put the children to bed and sealed the windows and doors against everything. Cyrene and I took her into the temple. John and Nick had left not long before this as they had driven back to Manchester. Leaving her with Cyrene I said do not let her sleep do anything to keep her awake I am going to cut the power off. Ok he nodded knowing what I meant some darker spirits will create diversions whilst they go for the target. The others had ignored graces incessant jabbering got on with what they knew needed be done to support me. I saw the slug creep under the temple door trying hide near the walls against the black, I saw it crawl up Adrienne saw it enter her at the back of the neck. I knew Cyrene knew what to do fetch her back to herself kill the larval slug. So, I was just about to leave the temple when the goddess Kali came through she said with your permission lady the soul eaters dance can begin. I nodded she entered me I sort of watched myself transform into her. The wreath of skulls about my waist the serpent hairstyle all hissing at once good job I like snakes.as two coiled on my arms hissing now I had four of them. It felt pretty strange, but we walked out there with a serpent's tail at the rear of me. I had spoken to kali before but never had she asked to use my body before.

Adrienne

I felt very odd like I was being crushed y this black slug taking all the space in my body's I ran into the head, my head hurt very much I couldn't see but knew they would get me back, Cyrene kept holding me blessings me with the sacred water from the altar feeding me something salty bread dipped in salt and red wine it made me feel worse he said I needed to push it out. Not allow it stay inside I did not like it so ran away from it, but it followed me calling my name. I needed the strength and warmth of Cyrene he was strong I felt his power surrounding me I knew I would be ok he bid me swallow more bread salt and wine it was hard then gave me more wine to swallow it whole. I wanted to be sick, he was doing it to make me sick. He knew if I were sick it would come away too.

Circe/ Kali

We had to call Adrienne back to her body through the astral she came but was building a castle wall between it and her. I took the sword cast a circle of blue fire around Cyrene and Adrienne this cut off the power from what was feeding the slug. Then I let me well Kali and I out of there into the lounge. L was now the soul eater this was my dance. Grace was having a debate with Hekomya he a demon of greater power. I placed myself between them sitting down, grace spoke to me saying hey we were having a debate here what are you doing stopping it like this.

Kali replied I am not Circe she is not here you will answer me now, decaying soul. Why are you wearing all those masks they cannot protect you from me for I am she who eats souls? You cannot hide your decaying flesh from me. I see beyond the skin to the bones beneath. Why are you holding this young soul in your belly ? Let it go and accept your fate, you no longer dwell with these creatures you are no longer one with them. But instead you try steal another form. Why is it that the outer manifestation is not the inner reality can you not hold it together? You are hiding right now but the masks are rotting and falling away from you. Your grip on reality is failing you come let the soul go now it cannot sustain you anymore. Grace began to stutter and panic, she kept calling for Ashna to help her.

Kali replied it is of no use Ashna is not here, but I am she who just is. Grace shouted I have free I can choose what happens here. Kali laughs no child you have gone way beyond human free will you are dancing with the very darkness of creation now. What is it you seek that I who birthed worlds? Cannot grant you , if you turn your face away from me then the only path left is Satan. The destroyer of worlds. At that moment he appears at the door, looking straight at kali. Looking then at the crouching thinking the corner choose demands kali.

You have free will, till, you choose the plane of extent in which you create your domain. Satan stood there watching the soul eaters dance progress. Grace spat contempt at the goddess kali saying she had no right to interfere here the soul was hers to keep hers to devour. It offered itself to me so it is mine you cannot take what is already devoured. I regret you are not listening asked what you sought to gain from denying your own death shades have no rights to claim a life at all. Grace spat, am not playing at devouring it I have devoured it as I am devouring that young thing in the other room.

Kali hissed as the serpents moved along the backs of the chairs having crawled from her arms, she said to Satan do you want it? Or do I destroy it here.

Grace looked scared now as she saw Satan walking towards her no, she yelled not him please I did not choose I did not choose. Kali laughed as the snakes coiled around her writhing and hissing she kept moving out of the way kali said to Satan take it but leave that young thing inside it for me. He nodded at her took what was already his.

Once the demon was gone kali said to Hekomya run the water add the salt and concentrate it this child must be washed take care of it. They agreed do so. Kali heads back to the temple falls half into the circle as a huge snake. Adrienne was back the slug disabled in salt. Still wriggling but shrinking by the second. Cyrene said it is done then. I came back sitting up saying did we do it. It seems so then into the room comes Hekomya carrying our grace wrapped in towels. Places her down she was crying saying she had a terrible dream a monster was eating her piece by piece. We laughed said it is the mushrooms dear mushrooms in the food.   do not eat any more mushrooms!

SONIA

Sonia had been in our coven for over 5 years taken her second level

She was an excellent herbalist and wrote sections of our coven notebook which was circulated monthly to keep our members up to date with what was going on. It gave them the next few dates for rites. So, if they could not be there, they could tell us, and it would be recorded in our coven notes. Sonia had decided to create a sacred room inside her home as some who are advancing do so they can then work more. She had affinity to Aries he was always turning up watching her.

One night not long after 10pm my rottweiler started to snarl I watched his ears prick up then he was sniffing the floor. He looked at me, so I followed the dog out into the hallway through the kitchen at the end of the kitchen was a door and a step. After opening the door my dog's teeth were bared, he was really snarling now he stood in front of me, so I did not step down. Right near our locked temple door which was just after the front door also now locked in the night. Stood someone who resembled Sonia. She or it was trying the door saying your portal is open I need to get into there. I said no go home we will deal with this in the morning its late now. My husband was upstairs in his man cave playing games he heard the snarling of the dog. He came down the stairs looked at our dog. Who woofed at him he came down opened our front door pushed her outside saying go home we will come see you tomorrow?

We locked the door again it must have gone back as we were not disturbed again, I hugged our dog kissing him loads gave him treats for being great. The very next day quiet early like just after Dawn as it was winter, so it was 8am or there abouts. We went up to see Sonia to find out what was going on here. As we drove towards the parking, we saw her crawling around the ground on her hands and knees, in her pyjamas no glasses no shoes at all. We parked the car went to her said what are you doing? She said I was out here I think last night I lost my necklace the pentagram I always wore. We said we would buy her a new one and walked with her to her flat. But as we walked up the stairs, I felt something was off inside her place. I said Sonia what is inside your place? She said oh that yeah it ermm came through the mirror, then it broke. What broke my lovely dark mirror the one I made at your home. What were you doing at the time? I was trying a rite from an old book I found. Which was about? oh demons and darker things I wanted know if it worked. Ok my high priest said so what is this room if you are sleeping in the lounge. Oh, I built a temple room in there. Can we see it I said? Of course, just go inside I opened the door we were not wearing shoes as like us she preferred no shoes be worn past her door.

As I opened the door, I saw something in the corner that looked terribly upset. I walked in it looked at me I said were you in my home last night it replied yes but you would not t allow me to the open portal you have there. No, I said why are you here? She invoked me but then she smashed the mirror I have been trapped here for 3 days. I need to leave. I said so her portal is broken, and you need a doorway opening so you can, leave. Yes, it replied. I said did she ask you for something? No, I think she was experimenting is all, she was shocked it worked. I said so you are from where? It said Lady you know already I need to go back help me. I said I will be back. Went to Sonia who had made us coffee and cakes, said the demon in your room wants to leave do you have another mirror? Yes, but it is not a magical one. No matter I said we need open a door so it can leave, then close it and break the mirror. Oh, she said well then, I will need another one of them as well I get dressed by the only other mirror I own. No matter we can go buy what you need; later we need to release this demon back to its own domain. Please do not play with them. You are lucky this one is a lower demon not that powerful.

So, we cast a circle the demon was inside it with us in a triangle we opened a magical doorway and allowed it to leave. Later we smashed the mirror putting it into the bins outside. We did not want to leave it inside the house in the event it might be able to be opened from the other side.

Whispers of the Witch by NanyWytch

In our coven we teach about magical doorways being reflective surfaces and to not have any in a room you are doing magick inside. We do have two dark mirrors inside our temple so the Gods can come and go as they wish. Plus, our guardian uses it mostly.

We took the book off our witch and said no more playing at invoking demons. I will give you some lessons on the darker side of magick as you are progressing to your 3rd level. I will expect you to learn from the papers I give you I will suggests a few good books as well. As you may want to read around the subject matter as well.

That sorted we went out to breakfast and to help find something we could help make a new dark mirror with. We spent most of the day with her.

Not long after this Sonia arrived at my house with a rucksack on her back one day she came inside, and we asked her what drink she wanted she said tea. Now we thought this odd because she did not drink tea at all. But we made a drink of herbal tea. She drank it whilst it was ridiculously hot. We knew Sonia hated hot drinks if she had herbal tea, she let it go cold first. She was behaving a bit odd and talking about having weapons in her bag. We asked her why she needed weapons in her bag was she not going to university today. She said no I have to go somewhere else stop them trying get me. She worried me a lot I was not sure if she had been playing about with the darker side again and something had gone very wrong. Or what. But as the day drew on her behaviour deteriorated. She acted very paranoid about things and claimed her family were going to harm her. We asked another covener to come to us whom was a psychiatric nurse. After she had talked to her she came to us and said she was worried for her state of mind thought she needed to spend a couple of days at the hospital. We were genuinely concerned about weapons in her bag, we opened it she had quite a few knives in its big ones.

We were not sure what to do but we asked Sonia about going to the hospital talk to a Dr there we had contacted. She agreed. But kept on saying her family were trying to hurt her, we knew her family were Mormon, and we knew she had not seen them in over two years since she had come to university. So why now would she think they were going to hurt her. We knew they tried to marry her off to a man a lot older than her at 18 which was why she had left them and gone to university in the first place. So, we asked had they contacted her she said yes threats in a letter its really upset me I think they know where I am. I need to get away. We said she could stay with us. No I don't want to involve you in my family disputes I wouldn't feel right about doing so I am not stopping being a wytch its made me feel very free indeed but my family will think I am possessed by the devil and want a exorcism so it scares me I don't think I can handle this I need some help from a Dr..

She was admitted to the psyche unit for an assessment a few days later we were told she had disappeared at night from the unit. They said they thought she was suffering from a form of paranoia caused by stress and anxiety and were concerned for her safety as were we

. After trying find her by going to her flat which was unsuccessful, we saw a lot of bin bags near her bin. All her magical things were in here as well as books and her book of shadows in fact everything she owned was here.

We took the books and magical tools back to ours and began to wonder if Sonia had been forced to go home by her family. We do not really pay much heed as witches of how other Christians see us. Especially those odd sects not the main churches. We like to think in 2020 we are advanced, but I have seen some very bizarre things during my life that say to me we are as a people so very primitive in some of our thinking. I do not care what people choose to believe. It is my concern that quite a few beliefs do not give an open choice to people. It is awfully hard to imagine in today's world that a girl of 22 years could be coerced to do something so drastic but then we do not think about these things and the way other belief systems view witchcraft.

May the gods bless you always?

HARDMAN STREET

Whispers of the Witch by NanyWytch

My parents were looking for a house in Blackpool to be nearer to us, mother and I went to see a lovely 6 bedroomed house in their price range near Derby baths. These were old Georgian houses, very nice indeed this one had a long hallway. Then front lounge, back lounge, dining room, breakfast room, kitchen and walk in pantry on ground floor. The lady was leaving all carpets drapes, and a lot of the antique furniture. Upstairs on first floor were 3 bedrooms nice large ones plus a bathroom. On second floor another three bedrooms plus a bathroom. Then it had one attic room.

Mother was smitten by this house, I said for the price I would buy it. Move here quickly. But father was different he had not been able to come with us that day as he was working. When we told him about it his only comment was no its too far from work for me. Mother laughed at him what one straight road; you could cycle it you know easily. No, he said I am not moving right up the north end of the town.

However, he did move up the north end of town by buying an old 3 bed terraced house right across road from work.

This house had a small vestibule then a glass door this small square shaped space became my girl's spaceship they drew switches on their nanas wall for up down go stop. They would run into the hallway peek into the lounge and say Arggghh no monsters run. They would squeal and scream as they ran back into their spaceship saying they were safe.

The house was genuinely nice the front lounge almost square with a blocked-up fireplace and electric fire. The back lounge was bigger and wider, but a bit dark as the light was restricted by a wall. Then there was the big kitchen and the yard. Upstairs were two large bedrooms, one small bedroom beyond a bathroom. It looked like whoever decided move bathroom upstairs to extend the kitchen. Had simply

Whispers of the Witch by NanyWytch

divided the back bedroom in half. Not thinking of privacy needed in bathroom.

Not long after they moved in mother talked to me about seeing spirits inside the house, she said a lovely lady who smelt of flowers like lily of the valley perfume. A teenage boy who was very nervous. Then a grumpy older male always in a huff,

On my first stay at the house we were dancing in the front room to music when I saw a woman walk out the fireplace to the hallway and vanish next door. The next time I stayed over I saw a man come out the fireplace in the other lounge. Walk outside light a pipe and smoke it looking over the wall.

But on my third weekend stay things jumped to far more serious, I was sitting in an armchair in the back room near the back window. My baby asleep in her pram outside in the yard. The family were all there my youngest brother then 13 years old was laid like a rug on the floor, my other brothers on one sofa dad in the other armchair. We were all watching a film father had bought called pet cemetery. Everyone was engrossed in the film. Suddenly without any warning the man mother had described as always being in a mood. Came into view he was rushing towards me with an angry look on his face shouting at me

So, you thought to come back did you Elaine, well I will finish you off properly this time. He grabs my throat standing astride me begins choking the life out of me. He was very strong indeed. I could not scream or shout, I struggled get free then stopped panicking and began to think I was going to die right here in the room at only 19 years old.

Then I remembered a move in karate where you are being chocked, where from standing you can move an arm over the top of theirs. Twist and it forces them let go now you kick them hard. I did this all my family saw was me stand up turn around and kick at the chair. Dad said oih you pack it in daft sod.

If only they could see what was really happening, when I talked to my baby brother, he said every night since he had slept in the back room. This really angry man has come in when he was in bed took off a belt and beat him with the buckle end. He had no idea why but he didn't call him by his own name he used another boy's name. He showed me red marks he had on his back.

Soon after mum wanted get a new kitchen and gas central heating put in the house, she wanted knock down the fireplaces make the rooms look bigger. So, they hired builders and the gas company. They were told it was a very big job, that floorboards had to come up and that they needed move all the furniture out of these rooms. To make the job quicker. So, my parents arranged with a neighbour stay over there for couple of weeks.

The work started but when the first fireplace was knocked through, a woman's decomposed body was found, the work stops the police come and they are concerned there could be more. So, the builders knock the other fireplace down finding a body of a man standing inside it with a rope about his neck. Under the floor right where the sofa had been the body of a skinny teenager was found. He had been savagely beaten to death

The investigation slowed up the work the first lot of builders refused return to the house. So, dad had hire new ones who were not told about the bodies. The job took in total 6 weeks instead of three. All this time my mum was sleeping with dad at Doreen's the boys were sleeping with Jens family as they shared her sons' room.

The police spoke to neighbours finding out around 8 years previous to my family buying the house a mother and boy had vanished when the neighbours kept asking about them the husband acted strangely saying they had gone away but weeks later he's not seen after having a delivery of bricks and mortar.

So, it seems our spirits were one family. Where the husband beats the son to death. Maybe the wife objected to this, so she was killed to cover up the other death. But in truth we will never know what occurred. After the work was completed the spirits had gone and did not come back. My parents lived here till they moved to Manchester.

Sometimes spirits only stay till was needed to be done is finished, others choose to remain. But those whom are stuck are normally those murdered, or those who committed murders.

Authors Note

Here we end my first book of my life.

I do hope you enjoyed what you read so far.

If you wish to know more visit my web site or email me, I am not teaching at present as I need surgery. But am willing answer questions arising from my book.

www.nanywytchwriter.co.uk

ashna@nanywytchwriter.co.uk

Blessed be may the Gods light up your life.